Dee McAlinden

Downloading Grey Thinking

First published by Createspace in 2017.

Copyright © Dee McAlinden 2017

ISBN: 9781540675354

Visit: www.deemcalinden.weebly.com for more information about Dee McAlinden and her work.

Disclaimer:
No part of this Book may be reproduced or transmitted in any form or by any means, electronic or mechanical, including photocopying, recording or by any information storage and retrieval system, without written permission from the author.
The methods describe within this Book are the author's personal thoughts, model, recommended reading and models and suggestions. They are not intended to be a definitive set of instructions. You may discover there are other methods and materials to accomplish the same end result.

Downloading Grey Thinking

A book that shares the models which helped me develop my AS mind that enabled me to communicate with Neuro-Typicals (NTs) whilst maintaining who I am, An Autie.

My own, my son's and my daughter's ASD diagnoses are all Level 1/Autism, previously know as Aspergers. However, I would point out that my own symptoms presented more severely when I was a child such as muteness at school and being extremely socially isolated up until my mid-twenties. Therefore, I recommend this book primarily for other ASD level 1 diagnosed/undiagnosed people, both children and adults. I would suggest also that level 2, with more support, could benefit from using the tools.

The tools in this book do not exclude Neuro-Typicals (NTs) therefore I recommend them for that population too, especially if they are coaching someone with ASD.

Throughout the book I will refer to the person on the spectrum as an Autie. This is an

affectionate term for someone with Autism. I do sometimes use the word Aspie (shortened from Aspergers) but feel that would exclude those of us who did not receive this label.
I will refer to someone who is not on the Autistic Spectrum as a Neuro-Typical or NT for short.

I would also like to mention I've written the book predominately aimed at an NT supporting an Autie, please ignore that if you are the Autie yourself. It was simply to make writing it easier for me. I learnt the tools and techniques myself as you might from this book. Also, if I write in a direct way that may seem too prescriptive please forgive me it's for two reasons:

1. My poor writing skills and
2. The way my brain works

Of course if you don't relate to a tool I've chosen, see the other resources I've linked or mentioned and/or research others you may prefer. The real aim is that the Autie is seeing the gap and then creating a concrete tool and practise to input into their portfolio. Learning consciously is essential for us Auties. I do understand we're all different and you may find my approach doesn't work for you, if so please pass the book on to someone else you think may find it useful. Please remember, it's written with a good intention: to help other Auties to Thrive with Autism and do great things during their lifetime.

Acknowledgements:

I have been very lucky to have brilliant, supportive people around me to help me get this book published. I'd like to recognise their wonderful contributions, I couldn't have created this book without them:

Ruth Milman - a kind, understanding and terribly knowledgeable person who has helped me understand my own ASD.

Paul - my husband and best friend who keeps faith with me whatever path I'm taking with a compassionate approach as all us Auties need.

Sean - my eldest and wonderfully brave young man who has forged his way forward into acting and encouraged me, through his wonderful example, to share my voice with others.

Amelia - my youngest outspoken, challenging, bossy, kind and extraordinary daughter who has told me "how it is" when I needed it.

Kim Goodman - a very dear friend who will help anyone who asks and with tremendous IT skills.

Jack Black - whose tools have changed my life over the past 20 years and who has created his great approaches with a genuine heart and passion.

Howard Childs - who diagnosed me a year and half ago. He listened to me as I poured my heart out reading from my papers listing my symptoms and has a wonderful interesting and respectful view of us Auties.

Alis Rowe - an inspiration! She is a trusting and loving person who has an amazing ability to explain Autism in a simple yet accurate way.

All the creators of the resources and tools I've mentioned in this booked and used myself. Thanks for creating these and sharing them so generously. Particularly Jack Black, (Mindstore), The Covey Organisation and Howard Gardiner.

Content

Chapter 1 Introduction to the Guide 8
Chapter 2 The Model Explained 11
Chapter Three First Meeting/Session 18
Chapter Four Decrease Anxiety 26
Chapter Five Increase Happiness 46
Chapter 6 Downloading Grey Thinking 66
Competencies Checklist - 153
Chapter 7 160
Appendices: 161

Chapter 1
Introduction to the Guide

As a parent of two late diagnosed children on the spectrum and being a late (48 years old) identified Autie myself, after the initial surprise, I have spent the last year putting together my own model of how I've managed to achieve a successful career, raise two wonderful Autie people, buy a nice, big house and sustain a happy life all with no interventions from support services and little help from friends or family (as I hide everything so well, this is not recommended as it has a cost to self esteem and physical health).

I'm now told that it is quite remarkable that I managed to achieve all these things with unidentified Autism. I know a lot of my success was due to my determination, inner strength and courage and the support of a kind husband (even though he did get it wrong, a lot, before my diagnosis) A sprinkling of luck also helped me reach this point in my life, for example getting a job in Human Resources which lead to a Learning and Development career. The latter taught me many of the "Grey Thinking" enabling me to communicate more effectively as well as many other thinking tools which I'll share with you in this book.

After the shock of my diagnosis (identification) passed, I started to work out the elements which I had managed without knowledge of my condition. These aspects of my life enabled me and my children to hold down jobs and careers, go to school, pass exams, socialise and generally lead happy and fulfilling lives. I then created a model to explain the focus areas and tools to address them. I think a model is important as it pulls together many tools in a managed process, which otherwise can be quite overwhelming. There are lots of great suggestions and ideas about how to help someone on the spectrum be happy, so I've aimed to make them manageable and phased through this model.

Through trial and error (and I'm sure this is will be a lifetime activity), I have developed an approach to parenting, mentoring and managing myself using the tools in this book. This book isn't going to have every answer, but I felt a phased approach from an Autistic person was missing from the book-shelves.

In the following chapters I intend to explain each element of the model and how it impacts on key areas of our lives in different contexts including, school, friendships, work life, socialising and life at home.

Here's the model:

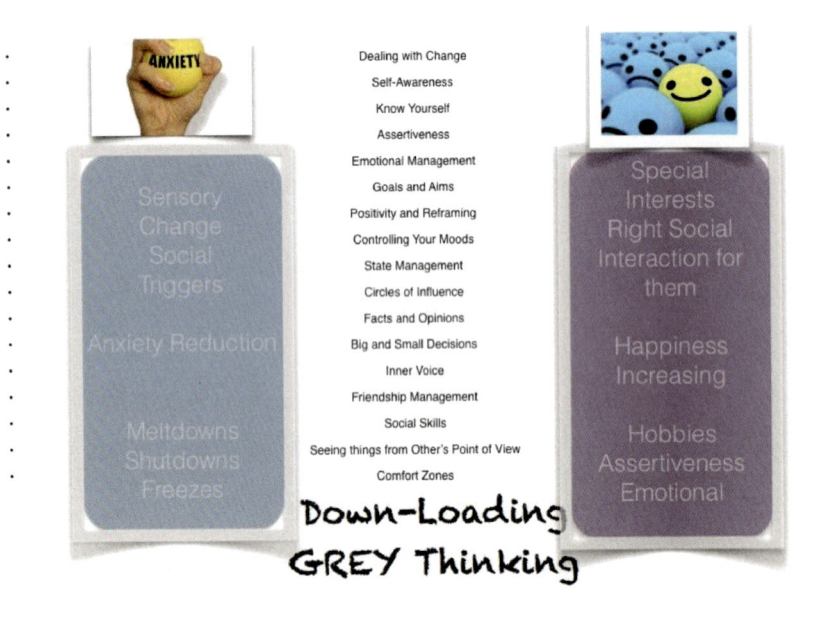

-
-
-
-
-
-
-
-
-
-
-
-
-
-
-
-

Sensory
Change
Social
Triggers

Anxiety Reduction

Meltdowns
Shutdowns
Freezes

Dealing with Change
Self-Awareness
Know Yourself
Assertiveness
Emotional Management
Goals and Aims
Positivity and Reframing
Controlling Your Moods
State Management
Circles of Influence
Facts and Opinions
Big and Small Decisions
Inner Voice
Friendship Management
Social Skills
Seeing things from Other's Point of View
Comfort Zones

Special
Interests
Right Social
Interaction for
them

Happiness
Increasing

Hobbies
Assertiveness
Emotional

**Down-Loading
GREY Thinking**

Chapter 2
The Model Explained

Since my own diagnosis/identification, I have been using the platform of public speaking to work through my own issues by sharing examples of ASD thinking and behaviour and by describing either what to do or what not to do to make mine and my children's lives' easier. Parents frequently have asked me to work with their children to help them resolve or minimise the issues of being an ASD person in a predominantly neuro-typical world. During my work with these children/young adults, I put together the model "Downloading Grey Thinking".

Many children I met or heard about through their parents were suffering from, what they described as, depression and felt stuck, numb, helpless and even suicidal. I noticed a pattern where parents and professionals were working on every issue simultaneously or just didn't know where to start which is overwhelming for everyone, especially the person on the spectrum. Everyone concerned can end up being bombarded with suggestions and tools from professionals which may help somewhat but can also feel like a drop in the ocean. Therefore, I created a model to allow the parent, practitioner or person with ASD themselves to isolate the key areas and work on them gradually and consistently.

What is grey thinking? Us Auties tend to think in black and white, that means: wonderful or disastrous; deliriously happy or absolutely dire; numb or in an absolute rage (meltdown). We can get stuck on one point and not be able to move on. We often have rules and processes and if they are broken by others we feel let down, frustrated and exasperated. We need to communicate that these rules or processes are important to us and why. This will help others to be able to honour our requests and/or we may need to accept that others may want to live their lives differently to ours and that this is OK as long as it's not causing anxiety to us Auties. The model and tools aim to address three areas:

- Reducing anxiety

- Increasing happiness

- Broadening our thinking (downloading grey thinking).

The first two elements, when addressed, stabilise the Autie so we can then go on to work with them on the "grey thinking".

The first step is to work on the anxiety reduction. Without reducing anxiety it is impossible for the person to start their grey thinking practice or learn effectively. I have heard living with ASD anxiety described as being in the middle of a war zone due to all the environment and social challenges we can face. It's no wonder we struggle to learn anything with that level of anxiety. This is absolutely right in my experience, we need to minimise the war zone by managing anxiety and stabilising the Autie person. This is both us Auties doing this ourselves, where possible, and with the help of the decision makers of the environments we live within and our support person(s).

Once you have started to identify and reduce the anxiety, you can start to encourage and even develop happiness through special interests, hobbies, relationships, good health and fitness and ultimately as much independence as possible.

Working on these first two areas will enable the individual to escape the anxiety and start enjoying their life. Anxiety triggers could be a whole host of things including: sensory over-stimulation or lack of; the number of social interactions encountered, routine change plus more. ASD is different for everyone. So an individual plan is required. I'd suggest you complete "Reducing Anxiety" and "Increasing Happiness" chapters first then review the behavioural competencies in chapter 7 to help you choose what tools to focus on first. Alternatively you can just work through the chapters and consume the information step by step.

Increasing positive special interests and hobbies will provide a counter experience to anxiety, giving the person a quality of life they need. I will share information about "safe" special interests and hobbies plus other positive activities the Autie can undertake whilst balancing independence and life skills which are essential for high self-esteem and confidence.

Whilst continuing to work on these two boxes (anxiety and happiness) as items present themselves you can start to work on the greyness issues in-between. These are placed in-between "Anxiety Reduction" and "Increase Happiness" as they are related to both, however, should be focused on only when you have stablisised your Autie first. The "Grey Thinking" work might be: the need to manage a particular friendship or assertiveness skills so they can say no or to reduce the catastrophising (black and white) thinking which is leading to anger, frustration or any other negative emotion. I have included some of the top tools I have used on myself, my family and clients over the past 20 years to increase my ability to function in a predominately neuro-typical world. This does not mean that I'm no longer an Autie, as I naturally think in black and white (which can be very useful) but that I think about my thinking and broaden it.

Using visual tools such as mind maps or pictures when you're working with the person is a good idea; you could draw the model and explain it. You could draw a mind map on triggers for example. I've put some templates in each chapter for you to use. However, if you have an equivalent that works feel free to use that instead, as long as you're working on the same outputs.

Reflection

This entire model encourages reflection which is not something we Auties do naturally. Therefore having a process to follow which helps us to reflect can lead to a change of thinking and behaviour. Many of the tools in this book require reflection.

Use of real life examples is very important to make sure the person can relate the model to their life.

If the person using the model is an Autie

If you're the Autie using the model for your own issues, it may help to ask someone to discuss the outputs with you to enable you to stay positive and to give you some examples of their grey thinking. You'll need to develop your self-awareness and be honest with yourself. If you do have a leaning towards negativity accept it and work through the toolkit to change that. It is ideal to work through this with someone with excellent "grey thinking" (Emotional Intelligence).

Parent or Professional

If you're a parent or professional using the model, aim to be consistent with its use. Plan a regular time to work on issues, weekly or fortnightly is a good timescale as it allows time in-between for your Autie to practise and not too long that they will forget what you worked on. Remember to make notes and create a file so you can review the last session and build a flow. You will need to ensure you are practising assertive behaviour yourself when working with your Autie. This includes:

Do

- Be calm and respectful towards your Autie

- Be curious and a good listener

- Be thoughtful about what level of energy your Autie has and therefore choosing the right time (regular appointments are ideal).

Don't

- Shout and exaggerate

- Tell them what they think

- Use leading questions (e.g. "Don't you think you'd feel happier if you practised meditation" – You're really telling them you expect them to reply yes and pushing them into your preferred answer)

- Become obsessed with the process so the output information (the gold) gets lost.

Point to note: A two-way respectful relationship is required. If your Autie is treating you in a disrespectful way, you will need to pick them up on this. Allowing this behaviour is wrong for a couple of reasons:

1. Your Autie is not learning good social skills and respect.
2. You are not helping them by ignoring this behaviour as they need you to push back some times. Not during a meltdown but in the everyday relationship. Just because someone is Autistic, it doesn't mean they can treat people badly. I speak about being thick skinned as a parent as you're likely to be faced with the anxiety when it's shown as anger, however, just ignoring this is ignoring the elephant in the room. It needs to be assertively dealt with: "That was hurtful"; "It makes me upset when you tell me I'm stupid". Timing is important here but doing this from a young age will help your Autie learn this early.

When and how long?

Weekly sessions are a good starter, you may be able to get away with every two weeks if you can't do weekly. In that case, have a slightly longer meeting and remember to go back over what you discovered/agreed last time and then build with the next step in the model.

30 minutes to 1.5 hours is where I would start. Younger children would benefit with the shorter time periods. You will have to watch out for your individual and see how they are coping with the time allotted. What you want to ensure is that the sessions are quality sessions and not too long.

Chapter Three
First Meeting/Session

If you are anxious and stressed this will be picked up on by your Autie, therefore, always aim to be calm and positive when working with your Autie. I cannot stress this enough, many parents I have met are so anxious about their child they are making the home environment uncomfortable and, I believe, causing more meltdowns and shutdowns. I've also met parents who are bullied by their Autie and therefore are walking on egg shells, if this is happening the parent needs to put more rules in place around behaviour. I remember feeling very anxious as a child at home (aka "the madhouse"). My parents not having control made me feel very insecure and unhappy. With my children I keep my composure and, when they're anxious, my sole focus is on finding a smart solution without blaming anyone whilst staying calm. There may be lessons to be learnt but during heightened anxiety or meltdown is not the time to do this.

Stay calm and confident and positive

Get to know the person's model (anxiety and happiness) but start with finding out their special interests and hobbies, this should break the ice. You could even take them to their special interest, watch an Ironman movie if they like "Marvel"; take them to an animal refuge or dog walk if they love animals (this is a very common special interest), you get the idea. This is about you going to their world where they are happy and themselves. Don't be scared of video-gaming with them!

Observe and Question – Be a Detective

Start to notice what's going on in terms of the Anxiety Box, you may already know this or you can find out from their carers/family/friends. Make a note of these by using the template "Anxiety Bubbles".

- Not knowing finish times
- Going to New Places
- Rap Music
- Waiting in disorganised a Queue
- Travelling on Public Transport
- Prolonged Small-Talk

You are aiming to find out what situations create anxiety for your person. You'll see in the example these will be things like: "travelling to school"; "eating lunch at school"; "going swimming"; "reading aloud". These will change during your person's life so it's a good idea redo every six months or so.

Don't expect to get them all down on paper straight away, this can be built on over time. Start off with one or two areas, usually the most anxiety provoking. Bear in mind the person you're working with may not know they feel anxious or be able to verbalise this so you or loved ones will need to observe or get them to draw pictures of the situations or use expression stickers to show you when they feel sad or anxious.

You will already be picking up what their special interests are which you can continue to enjoy sharing with them. Typically sessions with professionals often feel very serious (anxiety provoking for the Autie), so aim to balance this by including their special interest where you can. Having fun, building rapport and showing respect by listening to their input (words, voice and body language).

By the end of the first session, you will have started to get to know your Autie and be starting to build a picture of their "Anxiety Box" and "Happiness Box". You may also have picked up on any rigid thinking, lack of assertion or any other non-grey thinking they use, make a note on these for later, don't try and address everything at once (Remember you can start with the behavioural Competencies list in Chapter 7 to help you prioritise).

Important Methods/How to learn the tools Included:

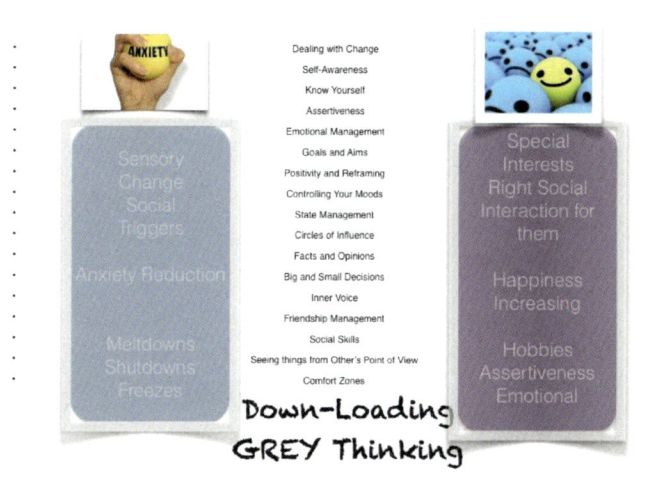

- Sensory
- Change
- Social
- Triggers
- Anxiety Reduction
- Meltdowns
- Shutdowns
- Freezes

Dealing with Change
Self-Awareness
Know Yourself
Assertiveness
Emotional Management
Goals and Aims
Positivity and Reframing
Controlling Your Moods
State Management
Circles of Influence
Facts and Opinions
Big and Small Decisions
Inner Voice
Friendship Management
Social Skills
Seeing things from Other's Point of View
Comfort Zones

Special Interests
Right Social Interaction for them
Happiness Increasing
Hobbies
Assertiveness
Emotional

Down-Loading GREY Thinking

How you cover these tools can be varied however we know visual and kinaesthetic learning tends to work well for us Auties. When working with your Autie by either explaining a tool, practising a tool, reviewing a tool, you'll need to use some methods other than just talking at your person. Here's some tools I recommend and use myself:

Social Stories (Carol Grey)

These are a way for an Autie to learn from a visual tool how to reflect, see emotions and the consequences they may experience. Carol Grey has developed many scenarios you can use to help your person understand the situation and it's consequences.

http://www.autism.org.uk/about/strategies/social-stories-comic-strips/comic-strip-conversations.aspx
For more information from the National Autistic Society about social stories see this page:

http://www.autism.org.uk/about/strategies/social-stories-comic-strips/comic-strip-conversations.aspx

http://www.aspergerexperts.com

Reflection

Reflection, I've already mentioned, is not something we Autie's do very naturally I believe, especially when we are young. This entire approach encourages one to one work with the use of real examples alongside the tools, therefore reflection is part of the toolkit. My own coach has reminded me of the importance of regular reflection (at least weekly) in order to check in with myself and ask how I'm feeling and how I'm managing my life.

Mindmaps (Tony Buzan)

I have used mindmaps for over 20 years for planning, prioritising, structuring, revising and designing. It's such a flexible tool which just requires one page or whiteboard. It can then be displayed to remind us of our output. When working through this tool kit you could use a mindmap to outline triggers or interests. In the "Filling the Grey" chapters you can use the mindmap to identify emotions or boxes in each of the four time management quadrants. Use it if you need to extract information from your Autie onto a visual document for review or reminders.

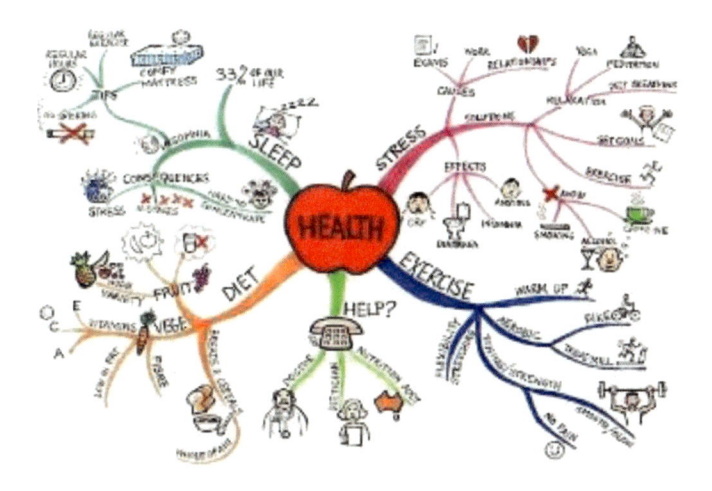

Here's an example, you can see the main topics off the central topic are: sleep; stress; exercise; diet. Then it goes into the details below each level and then details again. You keep doing this until you have exhausted all the content you want to cover. Starting with a big chunk and breaking it down to smaller and smaller chunks is something we Auties will definitely need to see. If you want to find out more you can buy a Tony Buzan book or search online:

http://www.tonybuzan.com/

Role-play

When practising social skills, role play is the usual way to do this. Whenever I've used role play in a business setting many people, although a little reluctant to start with, find it a very beneficial learning experience. I find if I role play the behaviour I want my Autie to learn and they can just act as themselves and then we swap they can mimic the skills very well. For example I, first, write down (plan) and then carry out the "Three Step Feedback" process playing the part of the Autie. Next we would then swap roles so they can have a go. You could do this with any of the social skills sections.

Analysis

Some of the tools you'll notice are analytical tools to demonstrate the current situation. For example social energy levels; time management; happiness levels and wheel of life. Analysis is learning in itself as the person may not know how they are feeling or how they're doing in a particular area of their life until they complete the exercise. Use analysis where you think it's appropriate.

Visual displays

Any way to prompt your Autie of the tool they need to learn or practise is important. Definitely keep key tools visible for example your schedule; plan; emotion thermometer. You can use other tools you create or find on the internet around the models.

Role Models

If you are working with an Autie you are a role model so please ensure you are practising what you are preaching or using your own mistakes to help them learn. If you're using this book on yourself, then aim to identify at least one role model for the tools. If you don't have anyone currently in your life you can use as a positive example, then look for the behaviours on TV or the internet.

Role models provide inspiring examples of the grey. Part of good grey thinking is understanding and accepting we're not always right and no one is perfect. I used to watch movies made for TV because they had lots of emotional situations that characters endeavoured to solve. I found this very comforting and educational.

On-line Courses

If you find other resources which help: use them. I usually firstly think about, 'what do I want to learn' and then I search for free resources. I've listed at the end in the social skills section some free online resources to use as part of your development plans.

Films/TV Programmes

Watching movies and programmes was always a great learning strategy for me, even though I wasn't conscious of my goals I learnt many skills like what to talk about with friends and how to start conversations. Aim to find programmes with integrity and linked to their special interests.

As already mentioned you can learn a lot from seeing behaviours and analysing the impact. Discussing these is a good technique too. Using questions on yourself or with your Autie at points during the coaching session. For example asking:

- What do you think that person is feeling?

- What do you think is the best thing to do here to solve that problem and why?

- List their personality traits.

- Would you like that person as a friend? Why?

Chapter Four
Decrease Anxiety

My two children have never had a meltdown, oh I tell a lie, my son went to a different childminder once and she gave him huge amounts of cola and he shouted and screamed at me for the first and last time. He never went back to that childminder. My son has probably experienced shutdowns or freezes when he was doing his A levels and certainly just before he was diagnosed when he failed his second year at university due to high anxiety and poor self-management skills. Fortunately, after his diagnosis he was given support and is now thriving at a local university and living a very happy and balanced life at home.

I, on the other hand, used to experience many meltdowns a week and a two-week shut down every February. This, I realised later, was mainly due to my high levels of unmanaged anxiety. My triggers were not being acknowledged and minimised and I was simply pushing myself too hard because of my inability to recognise my own emotions (grey) and my social energy (Alis Rowe's model) being depleted over and over again. Since my increased self-management, I can still socialise, work and manage my life without meltdowns and shutdowns and with decreased feelings of irritability and moodiness, a clear sign of anxiety, my life is absolutely wonderful for the first time ever!

Therefore, what do we need to do to identify anxiety and reduce it? The first message is that most people with ASD will experience Anxiety. Therefore the first step is simply to identify the triggers with your Autie.

STEP 1: Write down a list of situations that cause feelings of anxiety, which may manifest itself as aggressive behaviours, withdrawal, muteness or other behaviours. In my case I become very intolerant and lose my sense of humour. I also stop blinking and look scary I've been told.

A few of many situations that cause anxiety for me are:

- ☐ Going shopping at busy times
- ☐ Going to an unfamiliar place
- ☐ Singing in public
- ☐ Going to theme parks
- ☐ Socialising - going to parties
- ☐ Family gatherings
- ☐ Traveling to work
- ☐ My house being disorganised

Other common situations are:

- Lunchtime at school or work
- Travelling
- Unexpected visitors arriving
- Parties

- Going to a restaurant

STEP 2: Identify Triggers from those Situations

From the situations you can now identify the triggers, the specific thing that causes the anxiety. These may be absolutely anything! However they are likely to be because of: sensory issues (sound, taste, smell, touch, visual, balance and proprioception); change; and/or dealing with social situations. Recognise from the situations you identified earlier why and when your Autie becomes anxious. Here's an example of some of mine:

Situation   **Trigger**

- Theme parks - Queues (especially when you're not being managed properly)

- Traveling to work - Going to strange places, finding my way without getting lost

- Going to unstructured social events — the small talk, reading what people are saying and understanding and tolerating the small talk

- People in my home - People interfering in my processes (e.g. how I cook my rice, how I manage my home)

- People in my home - Extreme mess in my home, people not removing their shoes

- Family gatherings - Playing games involving timers, especially taboo.

Situation	Trigger	Solution
Going to parties	Small talk in unstructured situations	Say no to some parties Structure social engagements Role play small talk Give myself a time limit on the party
People in my house	People stirring my rice	Pre-cook the rice Ask them not to Keep visits short or eat out
Going to theme parks	Queues unorderly (people pushing in)	Get a fast pass (can ASDs may obtain these free of charge) Don't go! Distract yourself during queuing with radio, book etc.

How to tell if someone is Anxious

Sometimes we don't know how we're feeling (alexithymia) so we could do with as much help as possible.

- Physical signs

- Heart monitor

- Reflection

These are all good ways to check anxiety levels.

Types of Triggers

Sensory Triggers

You can see the music example of my trigger list is definitely sensory. I've noticed that when it's hitting my left ear predominately I go nuts! I don't just become anxious, I go straight into a meltdown. I once threw a chair across the garden because my neighbour was playing RAP music on his phone (which was tinny sounding). It ruined my entire day. After my meltdown I had to go and lie down. You can imagine, before we knew about my ASD these kinds of episodes in a women in her forties was frowned upon.

These triggers could be the flickering lights or the darkness in your house. You may notice the person avoiding parts of their home. When my husband messes up the garage, I can't go back in there until its tidy. I just notice I'm avoiding the room as it makes me feel anxious and stressed. Be a detective and be specific so you can identify sensory triggers and put solutions in place to prevent and/or minimise the triggers.

Social Triggers & Social Energy

When I don't manage my social energy (this is socialising and general functioning in everyday life), I have meltdowns and shutdowns. It took me a long while to stop being so tough on myself and to start pacing myself. Some people on the spectrum withdraw from activities that decrease their energy but that means they don't mix with the rest of the world and can end up frustrated that they are not meeting their potential in terms of career, financial, family, social interaction and ultimately in terms of happiness. How much social interaction we need is very individual but I would and do encourage my children to socialise.

Social for us Auties depends on what meets our needs. It could be meeting a friend once a week/month or seeing someone every-day. It could be through social media or face-to-face. As long as the person is happy and not feeling lonely and cut off from society you can rest assured they are getting what they need. Many Neuro-Typical (NT) parents put expectations on their Auties that are unrealistic and causing more anxiety for the child or person. As you can see from my list of triggers, unstructured social events causes me anxiety — what do we talk about, am I talking too much, is the other person bored (we find it hard to read non direct messages), when should I leave? Some sensory issues may be getting in the way of us socialising too, remember we may have heightened sensory issues and then we won't be able to hear the conversation in a busy place (echoing leisure centres and school buildings can be horrible).

Feeling invisible or shunned is a common comment Auties make. I felt this myself at school. This is the time when non-ASD kids are bonding with their friends and supposed to be the best years of our lives, however, it was the opposite for me and many Auties.

All of this will be draining our social energy and therefore making us more susceptible to a meltdown or shutdown. Make sure you include any social triggers and we'll talk about managing "social energy" later in the book (social energy, Alis Rowe).

Executive Functioning Triggers and Social Energy

All the things a Neuro Typical person does every day without thinking (using their executive functioning), us Auties have to think about. As soon as we wake up, every decision has to be consciously made — when should I get up; shall I wear my dressing gown, should I brush my teeth first or write my list of things to do? Little decisions feel as burdensome as big decisions and therefore anxiety is already there from the moment we open our eyes.

If something becomes disorganised I feel overwhelmed about tidying it up. I also feel angry that someone has messed it up as it's a waste of time to reorganise over and over again. It's messing with my processes to keep my world tidy and therefore keep my anxiety at bay. To NTs, this looks like I'm a control freak, I'm regularly called that along with competitive (I will admit I am a control freak, as I have to be but I'm not competitive).

Without finding ways to manage our lives easily, we will experience anxiety when our world becomes confusing and we'll have to keep on calling on our executive functioning energy (low already) to sort things out. We therefore need strategies so we can use our executive functioning on only the essentials and then refuel our social energy regularly. You'll see from my triggers people messing up my house or moving my things causes anxiety for me. I then need to really think about reorganising and therefore use my social again. Redoing the same thing over and over again when it's not necessary is also a trigger for me.

Time	Monday	Tuesday	Wednesday
6.00	Up and breakfast Dress, teeth, face and hair	Up and breakfast Dress, teeth, face and hair	Up and breakfast Dress, teeth, face and hair
7.00	Check bag & Leave house	Up and breakfast Dress, teeth, face and hair	Up and breakfast Dress, teeth, face and hair
7.45 – 4.30	Work Sean walk Hamish	Work	Work Sean walk Hamish
5.30	Home Prepare Dinner	Home Prepare Dinner	Someone pickup Amelia

Time	Monday	Tuesday	Wednesday
6.15	Clear up dinner things and tidy Amelia's room Check Amelia's piano and HW	Clear up dinner things and tidy Amelia's room Check Amelia's piano and HW	Clear up dinner things and tidy Amelia's room Check Amelia's piano and HW
6.30	Tutor	Time with Amelia	Home and Dinner
7.00		Marking	7.20 Amelia to Guides
8.00	Amelia's Bedtime routine	Amelia's Bedtime routine	Marking
8.15	Check School Bag Prepare Lunches	Check School Bag Prepare Lunches	Check School Bag Prepare Lunches
8.30	Lights out	Lights out	
9.00	Free Time – Quiz		8.55 Amelia Picked up from Guides and bed

Time	Monday	Tuesday	Wednesday
10.00	Bedtime routine	Bedtime routine	Bedtime routine

Keeping a schedule and diary here is so important to manage and monitor our energy levels for socialising, planning, functioning in day to day life without emptying our social energy buckets as this will cause anxiety, anger and meltdowns/shutdowns.

SOCIAL ENERGY TANKS ALIS ROWE (C) 2015

THIS REPRESENTS THE NT EXTROVERT. THEY HAVE A LARGE TANK WHICH IS FULL TO THE BRIM

THIS REPRESENTS THE ASD EXTROVERT. THEY HAVE A SMALLER TANK THAN THE NT, BUT IT IS STILL FULL TO THE BRIM

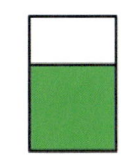

THIS REPRESENTS THE NT INTROVERT. THEY HAVE A LARGE TANK BUT IT IS NEVER ACTUALLY FULL

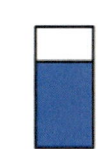

THIS REPRESENTS THE ASD INTROVERT. THEY HAVE A SMALLER TANK, WHICH IS NEVER FULL

I love this model by Alis Rowe, it took me a while to manage these levels as I wanted to keep doing it all and over-stretching myself. I had about three tests for thyroid dysfunction and one for diabetes as I couldn't understand why I had to keep going to bed for days on end. I now manage my diary more closely and ensure I have both types of events scheduled (losses and gains).

Losses	Gains
• Socialising • Social interactions • Changes in routine • Too much/the 'wrong' sensory input • Executive functioning/daily living skills • Feelings of anxiety • Ruminating • Poor sleep/exercise/diet	• Special interests • Hobbies • Alone time • Exercise/sleep/diet • Animals and nature • Meditation • Routine

At this early stage of working with your Autie it may not be appropriate to teach them complicated Time Management Skills but it is certainly a skill that will reduce their anxiety in the long run. I would recommend you ensure the daily and weekly planners are in place to reduce anxiety and then start to increase their time management skills once they have their stabilised anxiety and happiness boxes (see time management section in chapter 6).

Types of Triggers – Change

I thought I was a very flexible person before my diagnosis and felt frustrated and angry when people made contrary comments describing me as uptight or high maintenance. I do still think I have a laid back personality but I do have to manage change carefully due to my ASD. When my husband told me he didn't have holiday leave booked the following week during Christmas I blew a fuse and had a spontaneous meltdown in the car. My husband unwittingly sprung a change on me during the Christmas holidays just after a day socialising with the family. Again just knowing about my ASD helped us both recover but it reminded us that change is an issue I need to manage. Change does happen in life (otherwise things would be very boring) and so does expected change so we need to have strategies for this.

- ☐ Plan to avoid constant change

- ☐ Let us know if there's a change and why

- ☐ Tell us calmly and don't get upset if we do

- ☐ Create GOOD change surprises, which lead to happiness

- ☐ Give us a list of recovery things to do when we experience change

- ☐ Teach us that sometimes change does happen and it's OK, use a visual to show this like the example below. Then explain what we are going to do instead.

Meltdowns/Shutdowns and Freezes

I used to deliberately (subconsciously) get into a rage so I could use my executive functioning brain for tidying up, the surge of adrenaline helped me focus. My husband described it as living with a sergeant major. Not being able to organise and make decisions is very debilitating and affects our view of ourselves and ultimately our self-esteem. We can't work out why we take so much longer to do things. A trigger here could be feeling out of control (real or perceived) with homework or work.

You'll see this happening from time to time, but with diagnosis and management tools these should decrease as they have for me and my children. I used to have numerous meltdowns every week, now I've only had three in over a year and half.

Managing our anxiety will also help us to reduce meltdown/shutdowns and freezes. However, it's unlikely we'll never experience them again. If we do, when we're recovered, discuss what happened and learn from them. What was the trigger, how can we prevent/minimise this in the future.

Medication

Medication may also be a solution for anxiety. I took a low dose of anti-anxiety medication and feel more able, however, this may not be the answer for everyone. After six months I gradually stopped taking the medication and now I purely use strategies to manage my anxiety and therefore prevent meltdowns and shutdowns. I share these in the "downloading the grey" chapter 6.

Strategies to reduce triggers

Once you have identified your triggers you are then ready to start working on eliminating them or minimising them.

Some therapists' approach is to expose the person to the trigger and allow them to get used to it. Remember we don't have the same kind of brain as an NT, I will never get used to poor quality RAP music, it's not something I can switch off, it feels like the person is drilling into my ear, I want to stop them and I want to kill them! As you can see, I'm very irrational when this happens. It's better to find a prevention or solution for our triggers rather than expect us to get used to it.

Obviously I can't stop my neighbours spending time in their garden but I can wear ear defenders or listen to calming music in my earphones. I can create privacy in my garden when I don't want to see people. I can and inadvertently did, create a calm and neutral colour scheme in my home.

So, it's now time to start to think about minimising the triggers.

STEP 3: Identify the solutions to the triggers and communicate them

Here's a list of some of the things you can do.

Type	Trigger	Solutions
Social	Dealing with small talk	Create structured social events Teach some social skills through role-play, watching others Limit your social interaction time (leave the party early).

Type	Trigger	Solutions
	People near us	Limit where you can to preserve social energy
Use hood or headphones to minimise sounds and interruptions
Plan to go to places with people you feel comfortable with
Have a mental calming process to use.
Sensory	Bright Lights	Wear sunglasses
Learn to be assertive so you can tell someone politely you need to leave or the blind needs to be closed.

Type	Trigger	Solutions
Change	Something changes unexpectedly	Have a diary and schedule to ensure you are organised. Have a strategy of what to do when things change unexpectedly. Wear an ASD identify badge to advise others. Have a support person who can talk you through a logical process at the end of the phone.

Type	Trigger	Solutions
Executive Functioning	I am lost	Prepare your route by researching well before you are going. Use the little person on google maps to show you where you are going and what it looks like. Virtually travel there or do a real dry run. Have a tracker on your phone so a designated person can check you. Have this support person at the end of the phone. Have a list of actions to take to calm you down. Leave plenty of time to get there.

Type	Trigger	Solutions
Executive Functioning and Change	I have lots of boring jobs to do and appointments to keep but I feel overwhelmed on Mondays.	Write everything down in your diary. Including non-meeting things (your to-do list) Learn Time Management Skills. Give yourself some breaks. Use your Inner Voice to encourage and praise yourself.

During a Meltdown/Shutdown Support

If your person has a meltdown during a session with you then following these tips:

- ☐ Don't judge them negatively, note it must have been an overload. Are you doing too much with them too quickly?

- ☐ Ensure they are safe. If not herd them to a safe space.

- ☐ Use calm words, voice and body language. Soothing them. "It's OK, it will pass". Don't interrogate them.

- Understand they will be exhausted afterwards and will need recovery time.

- When it's passed and they are recovered use this experience to learn more about the triggers so you can help your Autie avoid the trigger or change the meaning of it in time.

Even with the interventions and knowledge I have used during my life, I still do encounter meltdowns from time to time (much less frequently). Shutdowns are less frequent when I haven't managed my social energy well enough. As a support it's important you are realistic about your expectations, it's likely we will experience them from time to time, especially if we are stretching our comfort zones (Grey Thinking Tool). Don't see it as a failure, it's just an opportunity to learn more about ourselves and learn more strategies. I've reduced my meltdowns significantly from 150 to just two a year. I will continue to improve my life as an Autie through awareness and more strategies. It's important we know that we have some control and it will grow with time.

Empathy, Understanding and Support

Once my husband started to take my condition seriously and began to help me rather than discipline me over my anxiety and meltdowns, my anxiety started to decrease and our relationship improved. It is the ultimate way to say you love and respect your Autie, you are saying you believe them, they are not being naughty or controlling, they are desperately trying to function in an NT world.

Chapter Five
Increase Happiness

Once you've started to work on the anxiety triggers and solutions you can continue to do so alongside "developing happiness". You will have started this when you first met or began to work on this model. Now is the time to find out more and encourage additional positive happiness activities.

You can firstly ascertain happiness levels. Ask yourself/your Autie to answer the following question:

On a Score of 1 to 10, how happy are you today. You can continue to do this throughout your work. Remember it's unrealistic to think we're going to be a 10 every day, life's not like that. However, we can be a 7 regularly. It encourages your person to think about this positive emotion and analyse what's contributing to their happiness or sadness.

Special Interests & Hobbies

Special interests could be anything, one Autie boy I came across had a special interest in cemeteries. Common special interests are:

- ☐ gaming
- ☐ space,
- ☐ trains,
- ☐ psychology,

- dolls,

- action man,

- collecting things

- Minecraft

- Lego.

My special interest as a young child was playacting the school teacher, this is a typical way for girls on the spectrum in particular to try to understand the social world and prepare for it. I also collected and played with rubber insects, I used to chew and smell them; it was very comforting.

HALLOWEEN 1987 "DEE"

As I got older I started to become interested in Marilyn Monroe. By the age of 17 I was dressing like her and by 18 I bleached my hair. This special interest was starting to become dangerous for me, not directly because of the special interest but because of the attention I received because I looked like Marilyn. It's important to allow a person to spend time on their special interest, it makes us happy, and it allows us to escape anxiety and to refuel our social energy. Later in this book I'll talk about staying safe when a special interest becomes an obsession and consequently potentially dangerous.

When parents tell me they're worried about the amount of time their Autie is gaming or to whom they might be talking,

I say, "Why don't you join them in their special interest". My husband and I used to play video games with our son, Prince of Persia was a favourite. He was with us socialising and we were indulging him in his (and my) special interest. If they are playing with strangers online again you can be involved. Also it's important to teach the risks and put some rules around this type of interaction.

It's always wise to prepare your children for potential dangers but it's essential for us Auties, we are very vulnerable and will need to be told what might happen and then what to do in various situations. More on this in later chapters on "downloading grey thinking".

One of my daughter's special interests (she has a few) is Miss Marple. We've taken her to a play and we regularly re-watch her favourites. It's been a habit of mine and both my children to re-watch our favourite movies, it's comforting, predictable and we enjoy them over and over again, therefore, don't criticise this habit if your Autie has it too.

Creating a safe and relaxing home environment has been imperative for my happiness. Nice muted colours create the sense of calmness I relish. Think about all the senses, the colours, sounds – I use relaxing music and switch TV and radios off if they are becoming too much; Smells – fragrant candles are an important part of my home now. Creating a tidy space so my mind can relax I have found extremely important too. Remember this will be unique for your Autie so try things out. Colour boards to plan or look in magazine. Go to a candle shop and spend some time smelling the scents, see if they have any impact. Search online for music or sounds your Autie may like.

Social Interaction & Skills

Encouraging Social interaction is important (I believe), in my experience, all Auties want some kind of companionship; even it's with an animal companion. It's equally important however to understand we do not need the same level of interaction as many NT children or adults. I've always found it baffling that some school mums spend the entire day together regularly, what do they have to talk about and I've always got so many things to be getting on with. Life with our animals and special interests can be wonderful. As we're behind our glass wall (Rudy Simone) or inside our glass jar (Elis Rowe) with most people it's important for us to trust our friends enough to be able to come out and feel safe and accepted. These special relationships are only with people with whom we feel comfortable to be ourselves. This is when we don't have to camouflage ourselves as NTs. We can say what we think or feel without scrutiny or being told we're wrong. I have close friends that I can be myself with but there are many that I put on the act with, as this is very tiring I can't keep it up for very long so I need to manage my social energy (see managing anxiety chapter for further explanation). Since applying this strategy, I've been very happy and less anxious. I go out with friends about once a month and meet for coffees about once a week. I walk my dog with friends around twice a week. The rest of the time I am with my dog or my immediate family which is ample socialising for me. I socialise on social media pretty much every day which is also an excellent way for us Auties to feel connected. It gives us more control of the duration and has no voice and body language to interpret. Word of caution that I'm sure you're already aware of, we need to stretch our comfort zones with communication with other Auties and NTs if we want to interact with and work within the mainstream. However, don't send us into panic zone (See Comfort Zones in Chapter 7).

You'll need to support social interaction based on how much the person seems to need. During adolescence many teenagers start to realise how different they are and how complicated the NT social world is. They may start to camouflage more or, conversely, refuse to and become socially isolated and perhaps aloof. There are pros and cons of camouflage (acting normal/NT) which you will need to be aware of. Just enough to get by socially in the NT world is positive, but the majority of time must be spent as their true selves otherwise we'll feel fake, confused and unhappy. This is likely to lead to mental health issues, especially if you're camouflaging without knowing you are (unidentified ASD).

Strategies

Do

- When they are young, arrange playdates on a weekly basis with school friends, one or two at a time.

- Build relationships with the parents (if appropriate) so your Autie can use you as a role model.

- Arrange events out around a special interest.

- Teach social skills early through role play and playing alongside your child (downloading grey thinking chapter)

- ☐ Talk about different characters' behaviour on TV, comment on acceptable and non-acceptable behaviours.

- ☐ Give your Autie down time to be alone or with their special interest to refuel/recharge their batteries.

- ☐ Be your Autie's friend. I have a very close relationship with both my children which I treasure, I pick up on their moods and encourage them to share if they need to. Being a calm and kind parent is extremely important.

- ☐ Use a schedule everyday

- ☐ Create start and finish times for activities

- ☐ Encourage their special interests

- ☐ Encourage other positive special interests (perhaps linked to a skill-set and possible career for the future)

- ☐ Teach social skills through play and good example

Don't:

- ☐ Shout and scream at your Autie — even if you're frustrated

- ☐ Use negative comments (always make things positive) for example say "what could you have done differently?" rather than "what did you do wrong?"

- ☐ Use sarcasm (unless, like my daughter, they have learnt what it means and are comfortable with it)

- Make comparisons with NT children or their peers.

Right Environment

Most Auties have sensory issues, either hyper (over) or hypo (under) sensitive or a combination of the both. I tend to be over sensitive to all seven senses (touch, sight, smell, taste, sound, balance and proprioception). This means life can be very unpleasant wherever we are. This will impact on our mood and anxiety levels and potentially cause meltdowns or shutdowns. Don't underestimate these. If you're an NT, you may think we can get used to the noise or the light or a whole combination after a while, like you do. No, we can't! That's why we have meltdowns, our brains cannot filter it out and instead of us getting used to it, it sounds louder or brighter or a harder touch and hence we run away and hide or scream and shout. When I was a child and my mum used to take me to Oxford Street by bus for new clothes, I always felt travel sick (on the 20 minute journey) and overwhelmed in the department store that I had to hide in the clothes rails to recover. I was not being a drama queen, in fact I was holding it together as best I could, but I'd be told off at some point for being weird or awkward or naughty. I still don't like shopping in a busy place, however, I am in control of my own time and can leave if I need to, shop on line and I can rationalise my feelings because I now know the grey skills of emotional awareness and management.

On the other hand a person could be under-sensitive and therefore be looking for stimulation of the sense(s). This may result in them banging on tables or windows or hugging strangers. We may also need both reduced and increased sensory stimulation at different times.

Either protecting the Autie from the sensory overload or provide the right amount of stimulation is very important here. There are many products you can buy to provide sensory stimulation and packs you can put together for protection like eye-masks and ear defenders. Ensure you are thinking about these things. Prepare a kit for yourself/your Autie that minimises the impact of over or under sensory issues. Mine is simply a pair of sun glasses, ear defenders (although I find them a little annoying) and warm clothing. Every Autie's kit will be different.

Here's some examples and links you can use to create yours.

EXTRACT FROM: Friendship Circle

http://www.friendshipcircle.org/blog/2011/12/13/26-sensory-integration-tools-for-meltdown-management/

Away from Home:

I suggest carrying a portable sensory toolkit for situations that may be stressful. Depending on an individual's unique sensitivities, some items in the kit may include:

- Sunglasses

- Baseball cap or wide-brimmed hat

- Ice-cold water bottle with a sport cap for sucking (or an ice-cold juice box with a straw)

- Chewy snack, such as beef jerky, raisins or granola bar

- ☐ Hand lotion or lip balm

- ☐ A piece of soft fabric such as velour for rubbing on hands, or a stuffed animal

- ☐ Squeeze ball or koosh ball

- ☐ Soundproof headphones (we bought ours for $10 in the gun section at Wal-Mart)

- ☐ Change of clothes (a long-sleeved t-shirt or sweatshirt and long sweatpants may be needed for tactile input)

- ☐ Carrier for child under 40 pounds such as Ergo or Beco carriers (ergonomically designed to distribute child's weight to parent's hips – my 4 year old says it feels like a big hug from me every time he rides in it)

At Home

When my son has a sensory meltdown at home, usually at the end of a busy day, I bring out the heavy artillery:

- ☐ Mini-trampoline

- ☐ Body Sock

- ☐ Silly putty, play dough or play slime

- ☐ Weighted blanket (ours is 8 pounds with a soft flannel backing) or vest

- ☐ Heating pad (very calming when placed on the back of the neck)

- ☐ Back rub or massage seat

- ☐ Ear, hand or foot massage

- ☐ Rocking chair, swing, slide or climbing structure

- ☐ Handheld massage ball

- ☐ Wooden foot massager (we keep ours under the dining room table to encourage sitting during dinner)

- ☐ Giant exercise ball for sitting and bouncing

- ☐ A favorite video or song (works best for under-sensitive people – I recommend the video Biocursion for its abstract images and music)

- ☐ Lavender essential oil or chamomile essential oil (one drop behind the ears)

- ☐ Chamomile tea (I mix in a drop of honey for my son)

- ☐ Massage jet for the bathtub (Pick one up on Amazon.com)

- ☐ Deep hugs or sandwiching between two body pillows

http://www3.northamptonshire.gov.uk/councilservices/children-families-education/SEND/local-offer/Documents/Children's%20OT%20SENSORY%20TOOL%20KIT%20home%202015%20FINAL%20VERSION%20(2).pdf

https://autismsocietyofnc.wordpress.com/2015/10/13/be-prepared-carry-an-autism-survival-kit/

Sometimes you have to expose your Autie to over or under sensory situations, so encouraging them to manage this themselves and feel in control is very important as they get older, they will need to understand how they feel, be assertive and organise themselves to be able to do this, these skills (State management, emotional awareness/management, assertiveness) are covered later in the "downloading grey thinking" section.

Healthy Lifestyle

Exercise

Being healthy and fit is clearly an important aim for anyone, it's not different for us Autie's. In fact, regular exercise is linked with good mental health and anxiety management and therefore possibly more important. This can become a special interest too. Alis Rowe (Curly Hair Project) is an advanced weightlifter and I myself trained to be an aerobics instructor which I continue to practise today.

Many schools insist on children playing team sports, I always hated being so close to people and was frightened by balls flying around during netball and rounders. Some of us have motor skills problems and therefore our eye ball coordination may be an issue. Balance can affect us too. Therefore, encourage your Autie to play team sports if they are keen and can cope with the interaction, otherwise, looking for lone exercise might be the solution. I started exercise to music classes at school when I was 15, it gave me some overdue kudos with my peers when they saw how naturally talented I was (a stark contrast to my poor netball, tennis, swimming etc. skills). I could have done with this positive attention much earlier in my school life. Some exercise options that could be observed:

- Dog walking
- Rowing
- Skating or Ice-skating
- Gym
- Dance class
- Virtual games
- Running
- Martial arts
- Swimming
- Yoga

https://www.facebook.com/nicole.zimbler

Food

Eating can be an issue due to sensory issues for many Auties. Also not knowing when we feel hungry or the opposite — never feeling full therefore overeating can be issues. I was a very fussy eater myself (I'm still somewhat fussy) and my parents and teachers used to make me eat food I couldn't stand the taste or texture of. I found mealtimes very stressful as there were so many foods that disgusted me. I did crave baked beans, peanut butter, roast beef dinner, curry, salad and spaghetti Bolognese therefore there were plenty of foods I could have eaten. My son doesn't like his food touching on the plate and I've always ensured it doesn't, it's easy enough to do. He also doesn't like cooked carrots so he has raw carrots with his roast dinner.

I encouraged both my son and daughter to help me cook from a young age, around four years old. We made cakes and puddings and then moved on to savoury foods. Consequently, both my children are competent cooks. I instilled the rules of nutrition as they learned how to cook very informally. My children now monitor their own intake of nutrition. Sometimes my daughter will point out that the drinks I bought are full of sugar and I need to change them.

Sugar can be an issue for many of us, as a child, I loved sweets and would eat everything in front of me until I was sick. In the 1970s we didn't have as much access to sweets but now this is a real issue for parents. I would suggest, as I would with any children, to put boundaries in place, teach your Autie this and stick to it. It's important to ensure there aren't too many temptations so don't buy sweets and cakes, just cooking your own sweet treats occasionally is far better.

Because anorexia is, sadly, higher than average amongst us Auties it's something we need to be aware of. I suffered from poor eating habits when I was a teenager and remember refusing to eat in front of people (I always felt so self-conscious) and mis-using laxatives. Luckily I didn't get to the point when I persistently refused to eat.

The research on this now suggests that there may be a link between ASD and Anorexia. I'm not going to comment on this as I'm not a specialist. If you have a concern about this please see your GP or a specialist.

http://network.autism.org.uk/knowledge/insight-opinion/understanding-and-managing-eating-issues-autism-spectrum

Do:

- Encourage cooking from a young age
- Make learning about nutrition fun
- Role model healthy eating
- Allow flexibility in foods due to sensory issues

Don't

- Force feed
- Obsess over food
- Buy too much sugary stuff
- Make comments about being "fat" about yourself or others.

Staying safe (avoiding sexual exploitation, drugs, alcohol, self-harming, negative special interests)

I was not safe in my adolescence and during my twenties, as I didn't have the right people around me. I was not equipped to make wise decisions about people and relationships.

In my teens I was described as a wild child as I was hanging about with the wrong people and following the crowd to fit in. This involved drinking, smoking and taking some drugs. I also drank excessively to manage my anxiety without knowing that was what I was doing.

"Downloading grey thinking" is about helping us to learn how to make judgements and have healthy conversations and friendships which is essential for happiness, by learning what this looks like. I just kept repeating the same actions over and over again. Making the same mistakes. I was very lucky I didn't end up in prison.

Some people have said I'm too involved in my son's development because I have been helping him to "download grey thinking" for years. You will need to ignore these comments from ignorant people who don't know anything about raising an ASD child and check your list of knowledge (see competencies list in CHAPTER 7) then start "downloading grey thinking" with your Autie person.

I mentioned earlier that my special interest of Marilyn Monroe became dangerous and how I got involved in crime and drugs and was a target for older men. My parents were sending me out like a lamb to the slaughter. I really think you need to tell your teenagers how other people will see them and help them recognise and avoid predators. I have explained to my daughter about stranger danger, this includes online as well as face to face. It's a balance of not frightening them but ensuring they know where risks are and what they must do to protect themselves against these dangers and what to do if they are at uncomfortable or frightened by someone else's behaviour.

Mental Health

Other conditions that often accompany ASD are something we need to consider and deal with. I think I have suffered from depression at some points in my life but since my ASD identification I think I've only had my anxiety to deal with. I believe the tools in this book will help to alleviate mental illness however if you suspect any of the following please visit your GP or psychologist.

Here's what the NAS have put on their website about OCD and Depression:

> ***Obsessive compulsive disorder***
>
> OCD is an anxiety disorder. If someone has OCD, it means that they experience repetitive thoughts and behaviours that are upsetting to them. OCD occurs in about 2-3% of people who don't have autism and is more common in people with the condition. It is thought that our genes (DNA) and our psychological predisposition can make us vulnerable to developing OCD, which can run in families. OCD can be distressing, exhausting and can get in the way of everyday life for the person who has it and their families. However, it is treatable.

There are two main parts to OCD: obsessions (thoughts) and compulsions (behaviours). OCD can be overlooked in people with autism as it may be mistaken for repetitive behaviour. However it is very different. If you think that you have OCD, let your GP know about your concerns. They will help you think about what to do and can refer you for a specialised assessment to help work out what may be OCD (or not) and what may be autism. Although there is increasing awareness of OCD, it is still under-recognised and therefore under-treated. If you have autism and think that you may have OCD, it's best to get an assessment and treatment by a team that specialises in both autism and OCD.

Treating OCD

There are two recommended treatments for OCD: Cognitive Behavioural Therapy (CBT) and medication. CBT gives you tools to help you change the way you think and act. As the most researched psychological treatment for OCD, there is now evidence that specialised CBT is effective for treating OCD and anxiety in people with autism.

Medication can be used either alone or in combination with CBT. The types of drugs that are usually prescribed for OCD are called Selective Serotonin Reuptake Inhibitors, or SSRIs. These include drugs like Fluoxetine (trade name Prozac) and Paroxetine (Seroxat). Some people with autism can be vulnerable to side-effects from medication and so it's best to start with a low dose, which you and your doctor can increase slowly over time if needed, monitoring your symptoms with an OCD monitoring scale.

Information about autism and OCD (psychoeducation) and social skills work can also form part of a helpful package of individualised care for people with autism and OCD.

MIND's website has further information about [OCD](OCD).

Depression

It is very common to have times in our lives when we feel a bit sad or low. But when these feelings last for more than a few weeks and get in the way of day-to-day functioning, this can indicate a period of depression. This is no different in a person with autism to someone without the condition. It is estimated that at least 20% of the population will experience a period of depression at some point but it is even more common in people with autism. People who are depressed can experience a range of symptoms which vary from person to person in their combination, and can be mild or severe.

It may be especially hard for depressed people with autism to seek help because they might find change daunting and anxiety-provoking, feel worried that they will be blamed, or feel unsure about how to describe their symptoms. Anxiety and depression can also make people more generally introverted, withdrawn and isolated. All people with depression may have difficulty sharing their thoughts and feelings. But because people with autism can have difficulty labelling their feelings, it can be especially hard to communicate symptoms or concerns.

Read more about the **causes and treatment for depression** on the Mind website.

Treating depression

Treatments for depression can be psychological or medical, regardless of whether a person has autism.

The most important step to getting help is for the person with autism to tell someone they trust, such as a family member, a close friend, their GP or another professional. Some people need a referral to a specialist service, either because they would benefit from psychological therapy adapted for people with autism, or due to a more complex set of problems.

Anxiety disorders, OCD and depression are just a few of the mental health problems people with autism may experience. For more information on other types of mental health problems, you may find it useful to visit the websites listed below.

If you have concerns about any of these issues please consult your G.P. or relevant health specialist.

Chapter 6
Downloading Grey Thinking

If you have followed the model and worked on reducing anxiety and increasing happiness, you're now ready to start working on downloading grey thinking.

Understanding our condition and highlighting the issues and challenges we face is the first step to downloading the grey, it helps us to start to know who we are and reflect on what's going on for us. Enabling us to work on the gaps and exploit our strengths.

This next model shows how the spectrum is very unique for each person and therefore knowing our unique strengths and challenges is very important.

Cartoon from "**themighty.com**"

https://themighty.com/autism-spectrum-disorder/

It's important to remember that our Autism will affect us in different ways and so we'll have different "Grey Thinking" needs. Some of us will have better listening skills than others and so on.

By reducing anxiety & increasing happiness (the earlier stages of this approach) we will already have started to allow our strengths to shine through and minimised some of our challenges. However, through "downloading grey thinking" we can address these further. That's why in this part of the book we will start to get down to the knowledge, skills and behaviours that us Auties need to learn consciously through getting the right information and models which explain (ideally visually) some of the broader world approaches to situations.

In the section we will cover:

- Dealing with Change

- Self-Awareness

- Know Yourself

- Assertiveness

- Emotional Management

- Goals and Aims

- Positivity and Reframing

- Controlling Your Moods

- State Management
- Circles of Influence
- Facts and Opinions
- Big and Small Decisions
- Inner Voice
- Friendship Management
- Social Skills
- Seeing things from Other's Point of View
- Comfort Zones

Filling in the Grey means broadening our thinking. I believe this is one of the ways I've been able to function and succeed in my career, relationships and home life. I was fascinated by what I learned during my career as a Learning and Development professional and by training other people it reinforced the tools over and over again. Let's have a look at some the top tools and skills I think are important for us Auties to consciously learn.

Dealing with Change

Change is part of life and something we must deal with. It's challenging because we find it unnecessary, confusing and scary. Therefore, we must be sensitive about our Autie and how to help them deal with both planned and unplanned change.

Ensuring we have structure will help us to feel more secure and therefore happier. I believe I'm more able to deal with change when it's not happening due to bad or lack of planning. If my life is ordered and organised and I'm managing my time through my schedule, my diary and my list of things to do then I can plan the change. Being involved in it, staying positive and understanding its benefits helps me to feel excited and prepared. When unexpected changes occur, it can be very frustrating however using my inner voice to calm myself down, explain to me that these things happen and I'm just going to take one step at a time (break things down) whilst managing my state helps me to get over the inconvenient bump (all these tools are explained later).

For example: When I decided to take the bus to a meeting and the bus didn't turn up and I was already anxious as I was meeting the SENCO at my daughter's potential secondary school. I didn't deal with the situation as well as I could have. I became very cross because the bus didn't arrive and I now had to make a new plan and make decisions which seem overwhelming when anxiety was high. I did make the decision to take the car in the end but the whole experience was not enjoyable and I didn't express myself during the subsequent meeting as well as I might have if the bus had come or I had managed the situation better. Here's an example where I managed these situations very well:

I was giving a "talk" and realised that someone had removed my laptop charger from its case, which meant it was at home. I had to think quickly, staying positive and asking myself the questions: how can I fix this, what's the worst thing that can happen? Telling myself: You can do this. I stayed calm whilst meeting and greeting the delegates, and asked if anyone happened to have a charger (they didn't).

I managed my state, choosing to remain positive and enthusiastic. I set-up the equipment I did have. I then explained the situation to the group, used the equipment as long as I could (20 minutes) and then used the white board and myself to deliver the rest of the event. I achieved outstanding positive feedback so was very happy. I asked myself what could I learn from what happened and, of course, it was to always check the entire kit from now on. In this situation I used some of the grey tools in this book to stay in control and manage the situation positively.

Forewarning us that change is part of life and sometimes things do happen which are unwanted and inconvenient, you could use a visual for this situation a "whoops" sign or change card to help us learn this. I have found, if the person I'm with is calm, confident and quickly creates a plan to get us on track or a safe alternative, I can move on. We then learn this from others so we can resolve unexpected changes using:

- ☐ Positive thinking

- ☐ State Management

- ☐ Logical thinking processes which focuses on solutions

- ☐ Reflection to prevent this happening again if possible

Equipping us Auties with a list of prompts on portable cards or phones is a good idea too.

For example:

What to do if the bus or train doesn't arrive on time:

- ☐ Take a deep breath and say to yourself, "I can deal with this situation"

- ☐ Check the live time service on your phone for updates, if the bus is delayed for less than 15 minutes, wait for the bus

- ☐ Call your support (parent or responsible person) if you are really anxious about the change for reassurance

- ☐ Wait for the bus, if it turns up within the 15 minutes get on and continue on your journey

- ☐ If it doesn't turn up check your phone again for live updates, if it's going to make you too late for your event, decide if you should take another mode of transport (train, car or bicycle) that you thought about when planning this journey

- ☐ Start to put in place your new plan

This example may be too advanced for your Autie so tailor these types of prompt cards for your person perhaps use visual prompts or fewer key words.

Self-Awareness

Before I reached my mid-twenties I would describe myself as an acorn, with so much intelligence locked inside. The transition from acorn to oak tree really started to happen when I began to reflect on my life and self: who was I, what were my strengths, what did I want from life. I wanted to be an actress and singer when I was younger but had no ability: to communicate this; few self-management skills; and was so anxious that I couldn't fulfil my dream. What a waste of talent! That is why it's so important for us Auties to spend time developing our emotional intelligences (inter and intra intelligences). Howard Gardner's model below shows eight intelligences.

Howard Gardener's Intelligence Model

Gardiner's theory explains that everyone can have natural strength in one or more of these intelligences however everyone can develop them too. Many of us Auties don't have good interpersonal and intrapersonal intelligences and even kinesthetic intelligences may present problems for us. We have to learn the emotional intelligences conscientiously.

Emotional intelligence is a combination of interpersonal and intrapersonal intelligence. You will see how we can and do really struggle here. Knowing your own emotions, self-motivation and working with people is where we really can fail due to our differences in reading people and understanding the NT world. On the other hand our naturalistic and logical intelligences can easily surpass non-Auties (NTs).

This is what the "downloading grey thinking" is. It's developing the emotional intelligences. Knowledge of this model and where are strengths and development needs lay is development in itself. You can explain the intelligences to your Autie as part of their self-awareness.

Know Yourself

Draw a picture of yourself and write down a list of characteristics associated with you. Here's mine:

- Energetic

- Fun

- Ambitious

- Adventurous

- Brave

- ☐ Strong

- ☐ Feisty

- ☐ Caring

- ☐ Generous

- ☐ Quick

- ☐ Impatient

- ☐ Logical

- ☐ Clever

Knowing how autism effects our characteristics is important too. Remember we have a personality along with our wonderful Autie brain. Autism makes me:

- ☐ Quick

- ☐ Logical

- ☐ Impatient

Sometimes my autism and my personality conflict. For example I consider myself to be laid back, I like to entertain and meet new people but my autism can't tolerate mess and loss of control so I don't socialise as much as I would like to and when people come to stay, I find it stressful as well as enjoyable.

Knowing your likes and dislikes is also a good exercise to do for improved self-awareness. Just put a line down the middle of a page and write likes and dislikes at the top. None are right or wrong it's your Autie's list. Here's an example:

Likes	Dislikes
Wild swimming	Queuing
Zumba	Crazy golf
Good coffee	People walking slowly
Gardening	People walking into my personal space
Aromatherapy oils and massage	

You can write as many things here as possible, it can be confidential if the person doesn't want to share it. Its purpose is for your Autie to think about who they are and what they enjoy in life and what they don't. It helps us understand ourselves, see ourselves as others see us and enjoy our own personalities more.

Assertiveness

What does assertiveness mean? It means being able to share our thoughts and feelings to others whilst being respectful. It's having respect for ourselves and others and being able to communicate that respect through our words, voice and body language. Once we learn a way to do this we can start to reflect on our own thoughts and feelings and then go on to structure it and communicate it in a positive and constructive way.

Let's have a look a couple of tools to help us do this.

Franklin Ernst's OK Carole

You are okay with me

	I am not OK You are OK *The One-down position* *"I wish I could do that as well as you do."*	I am OK You are OK *The Healthy position* *"Hey, we're making good progress now."*
	I am not OK You are not OK *The Hopeless position* *"Oh this is terrible – we'll never make it."*	I am OK You are not OK *The One-up position* *"You're not doing that right – let me show you."*

I am not okay with me ← → I am okay with me

You are not okay with me

You can explain to your Autie that it is important to think positively about ourselves and others at all times, even if we disagree. The OK Corral Tool (Franklin Ernst) is highly visible and you can talk through why mutual respect is important and if it's not practised it will impact on the quality of our relationships and life. If you explain each position one by one using examples of relationships, you can show the situation that arises. For example: if I think I'm OK but think Suzie, my neighbour, is NOT OK it means I don't respect her. There is a difference between "like" and "respect". Explain this difference as: If you like someone you'll want to spend time with them, find them interesting or entertaining or positive, it's a personal opinion. Whereas, if you respect someone it means you appreciate their strengths (everyone has them) and will behave respectfully to them (politely) but you may or may not like them, it's not essential.

I had a boss, who will remain unnamed, who I really did not like, I thought she was manipulative and a poor leader and every-time I saw her my "I'm OK, You're NOT OK" position kept affecting our relationship and forcing me into a negative emotion (anger or frustration) so I changed my position of her mentally. I thought about her positives. She was very experienced and someone I definitely wanted on my side. From then on I was more relaxed and genuine with her and felt a change in our relationship for the better. This does not mean that we become weak and allow someone to walk all over us, we still need to practise assertive behaviour. However, it does put us in a position where we are more likely to be able to respond assertively.

Another way to think of this is the PUSH/PULL Assertive Model above.

Being able to stay above the RED line in the green boxes helps us to maintain respect for ourselves and others, even if they have done something we're not happy about. It means we can say how we feel and what we think without aggression or submission. Remember the section on the anger triggers? You can see how these work together. If one of our standards has not been met we could go into red or even yellow and hold it (the negative emotion) all inside. It's healthy to say that we're not happy and why if we feel we have a right to the standard that has been violated (standards are explained in "know your emotions" later in this chapter).

	Push	Pull	
	Assertive	**Assertive**	
Above the RED line	Tells, Informs of own thoughts and feelings.	Question and listen to others' thoughts and feelings	Shows respect to selfd and others (I'm OK, you're OK)
	Keep these in BALANCE to achieve assertiveness		**Rational**

	If you: Push only, say nothing or pull too much your communication is NOT in balance and therefore Aggressive; Passive or a bit of both		**Irrational**
	Aggressive	**Passive/Submissive**	
Below the RED line	Shouting Overly forceful Angry Raise voice/angry body language	Quiet Speak too quietly Cry Look down Run away Allow themselves to be bullied	Shows disrespect for self and others (All other positions of the OK Coral)

Push/Pull Assertive Model

I've also added the Three Step feedback tool which helps us to practise the assertive push/pull box. Remember we want to aim for balance of these two green boxes overall, a balance of saying what we think and feel and asking and listening to what the other person thinks and feels. Sometimes we may do more green telling (push) and sometimes more listening (pull). Practising this with your mentor/coach or support will help you to find a pattern to explain how you feel and think. I've included a section on listening and questioning below so you can practise the green Pull side of the model too. Remember to write down what you're going to say before you practise it.

The third tool, "Three Steps", allows us to think about and structure of the content (message) that we want to communicate. This three step process has been extremely useful for me in my life. I remember when I was running a training programme a couple of years ago and I couldn't work out what I was annoyed and frustrated about so I got out my time trusted process and everything became clear. The next day I used the output with the person I was frustrated with and he apologised and improved his behaviour immediately.

Here's the model with an example below:

1. Say what you've noticed

"Yesterday when you were fifteen minutes late for the cinema...."

2. Say the impact it's had on you/think it will have on you

"It made me really anxious and cross as I didn't know when you were going to arrive or if you were coming….."

3. Say what you want them to change/explain/do differently

"Next time can you leave early so you avoid being late, or text me on route so I know when you'll get here."

This three step tool helps us to think logically, rationally and clearly about what the behaviour has been that we found challenging, how we felt or what we thought about it and finally a suggestion to improve things for the future. It's important we stay in the "I'm OK/You're OK" box when we deliver this message otherwise we will come across as behaving aggressively or passively.

Saying No

The simplest assertive message is saying "No!" Saying it respectfully but firmly. Here's the approach I use:

You may wish to include the entire three elements, although they are not all essential every-time.

Polite Ways to Say No

1. Make a statement of regret whilst making it clear it's a no.

(I'm sorry…, I'd really like to, but…I appreciate the offer, but…, etc. I cannot do this)

2. Explain why the answer is "No".

(I'm really busy right now, we're not available that weekend, etc.)

3. Offer an alternative, if possible

(I might be able to do it next week, John might be able to help you with that, etc.)

Discuss with your Autie some of your own examples and some alternative phrases you can use so they feel comfortable.

You will always need to make it clear that it's a "No", however, you don't always need to share why and offer an alternative. You might just do one of these two. Or if you have said "No" already and are still being asked you can just use a straight "No".

In extreme situations you may need to use the "broken record" technique. This is repeating No politely but consistently. Some people will try to push us into a "Yes" by persistently asking. In this case you can just stick to saying "No" and not explaining why or offering an alternative if you did these the first time.

In situations where you are at risk of abuse, the polite message goes out the window. You are entitled to be angry and do whatever you need to do to remove yourself from that situation that is within the law.

Some more examples here:

Polite ways to say "No" to a request

I'd love to help you, but right now I'm really busy with…I wish I could, but right now I need to focus on…Normally I'd be able to, but right now I have to….

Polite ways to say "No" to an offer

I appreciate the offer, but…That would be great, but I'm already working on…Thank you for the offer, but my schedule is full at the moment.

Polite ways to say "No" invitations to social events

That sounds great, but….I'm sorry I can't that night. I have to….I really appreciate the invite, but…

Time Management

Self-Management is controlled by our Executive Functioning, regularly a weakness for us Auties especially when our anxiety is high. Therefore, we can be very poor at managing our time. I found Stephen Covey's Four Quadrant model a very helpful way for me to think about what I'm doing and when. Here's the model:

This Tool can be found in Stephen R. Covey's book, The 7 Habits of Highly Effective People, I highly recommend reading this book.

The Time Matrix®

	Urgent	Not Urgent
Important	**I** **Fire Fighting** Crises Pressing problems Deadline-driven projects	**II** **Quality Time** Prevention, capability improvement Relationship building Recognizing new opportunities Planning, recreation
Not Important	**III** **Distraction** Interruptions, some callers Some mail, some reports Some meetings Proximate, pressing matters Popular activities	**IV** **Time Wasting** Trivia, busy work Some mail Some phone calls Time wasters Pleasant activities

© Copyright Franklin Covey Co. All rights reserved. Used herein with permission.

Covey categorises things to do into four:

Q1: Urgent and Important

Q2: Non-Urgent and Important

Q3: Urgent and Non-Important

Q4: Non-Urgent and Non-Important

Before seeing this model I didn't think of Urgent and Important as different. It was quite a lightbulb moment for me to realise I didn't have to jump whenever someone said something was urgent to me. Something Urgent means it has an imminent timescale linked to it and Important means it's going to impact negatively on you and/or others who are important to you if the task is not dealt with/completed.

Therefore Q2 is the box we should be spending most of our time in since if it's not dealt with calmly when we have the time to put the best solutions in place, it will move into Q1 box. People who allow Q2 to slide into Q1 are procrastinating and creating stress for themselves. They will be extra anxious. People who are spending time in Q3 are not assertive enough to say no to other people's priorities and if you're spending a lot of time on Q4 tasks, you'll be wasting a lot of time. I really like this simple and logical tool to help me prioritise my tasks.

Once written down I proceed to the next stage of prioritising my list of tasks into the four quadrants. This should eliminate some things (some of Q3 and all of Q4). I now have my prioritised "To Do" list.

I use a To Do list along with a diary. By putting tasks straight into my diary, it commits me to them. For example if I need to prepare for a public speaking event I know that is a Q2 task, unless I've left it so late it's become a Q1 task. Either way I need to prioritise this, so I will make space in my diary and set it as a meeting with myself to complete it. This works very well for me.

In addition to my "To List", I have my schedule which takes up time every day, however, I make sure I have some time during the day/week to complete tasks which are not on the schedule. See Schedule example in Chapter 4.

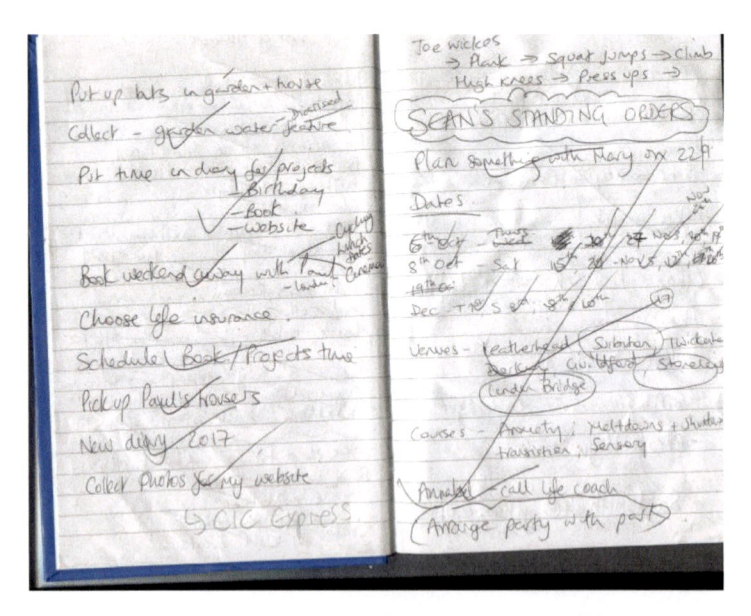

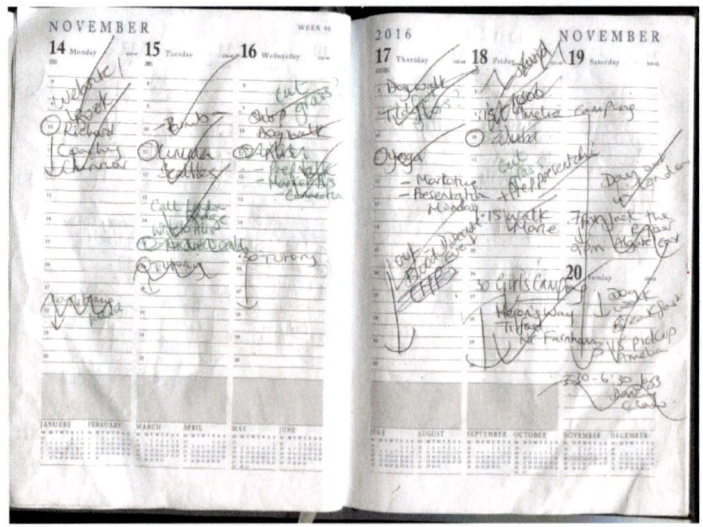

Once you have this process in place, reviewing your diary every week and then a smaller check every day is an important habit to enable us to keep on top of our commitments, feel we are making progress, have purpose and feel some control over our lives. Ticking the items off when they completed seems to be a common desire of us Auties, it gives real closure and satisfaction.

Problem Solving

Problem is a very negative word, we can change this to challenge Solving. Everyone has challenges to overcome, how to get a job, how to find a location we're travelling to, how to pass an exam. If we don't manage how we solve these challenges we may end up putting them off or avoiding them altogether. We Auties want to lead fulfilling lives so being able to manage our time and solve these challenges is important. There are many problem/challenge solving processes. Let's take a look at a simple and straightforward one:

There are four basic steps in solving a problem:

1. Defining the problem.
2. Generating alternatives.
3. Evaluating and selecting alternatives (prioritising which ones would work best).
4. Implementing solutions.

As you can see problem solving is, simply put, asking and answering questions you set. The process gives you a framework to do this that leads to positive actions to solve something. Here are some other questions you can see answers for as part of your process:

Ask Yourself	Example Answers
What do you want to solve?	I would like more meaningful relationships
Why do you want to solve it?	I think I'd be happier with more relationships
What have I already tried?	I've tried to arrange meet up but they haven't always worked out
What other suggestions do I have?	Join a club linked with my special interest
	Learn some social interaction skills
Who can help me?	My friend, Jessica
When am I going to do this?	Start meeting friends by May 2016 and review progress in Jan 17

When you have learnt some grey linking skills you can test your abilities by using problem to solve. Here's some examples below to try out:

PRAGMATIC QUESTION INSERTS FOR EASTER EGGS

- Your friend seems mad at you and you do not know why. What should you say to your friend?

- You are really upset about something and want to scream. How can you calm yourself down?

- You forgot your lunch! What can you do so that you do not go hungry?

- You lost all your pencils and class has started. How do you solve this problem?

- You got a bad grade on a test, and you are afraid you will be in trouble. How do you tell your parent?

- What would you do if you saw someone stealing something from a store?

- You see a classmate making fun of a friend. How do you handle the situation?

- You can't remember what the homework assignment is for tonight. How can you find out what to do?

- The lunch lady accidently gave you the wrong lunch. What do you do?

- Your test is really hard and you're overwhelmed. Should you just give up and stop trying? Explain.

www.livespeaklove.com

Saved from
livespeaklove.com

[Colette Schwartzman](#) saved to [social skills](#)

Emotional Management

Knowing how we feel is something NTs may take for granted. However, for me and my children it's like being numb along with extreme anxiety at times. We don't even know why we feel anxious . Anxiety causes ill health both physically and mentally. It's important for us to understand how we feel so we can do something about the issue that's causing the negative emotion (problem solve it). Many of us Auties have Alexithymia, Emotional Blindness. Here's a link for more information with an online test too.

http://www.alexithymia.us/test-alexhtml

I'm pretty sure I have alexithymia, feeling numb or disconnected from my emotions and then suddenly they can catch up with me. That's why conscientiously learning to reflect regularly, daily or at least weekly on what emotions may I be feeling or trying to process is good practise. Adapting this process will take some time, don't expect to read about emotional intelligence and management and get good at it instantly, I still trip up at times. However, I have a solid process I learnt from Tony Robbins that I use. Unfortunately I couldn't get permission to include his model in my book so here's another resource from Claire De Boar that will be useful.

Here's a great article by Claire De Boer about helping us to understand and deal with our emotions. Are emotions are there to help us in live but can often we can get stuck. Other tools in our book will enable us to process them more effectively, self-fulfilling prophecy; state management; positivity; 3 positions tool; however, really examining what's going on for us and then working through them logically will be essential.

How To Stop Being A Slave To Your Emotions

By [Claire De Boer](#)

1.

2.   "I don't want to be at the mercy of my emotions. I want to use them, to enjoy them, and to dominate them." ~ Oscar Wilde

3.   Would you describe yourself as emotional?

4.   Do you feel like your mood can change instantly according to what happens in your day?

5.   Then you may be a slave to your emotions.

6.   Being an emotional person and leading with the heart can both be great qualities. Leaning into our feelings allows us to be more self-aware and helps connect us to others. But if we allow our emotions to dictate how we live our lives, it can lead to anxiety, depression, and even have a negative impact on our health and relationships.

7.   As an empathetic person who feels things deeply, I have learned this lesson the hard way.

8.   It took me many years to grasp the concept that all emotions stem from thought. As a young woman with low self-esteem, I didn't realize that my negative self-talk and sensitivity to others' opinions were having a profound effect on my emotions and moods.

9.   After years of faulty thinking about who I was and what I had to offer in life, I found myself in my doctor's office clutching a prescription for anti-depressants. My emotions had officially taken control of my life.

10.   At the time I had no idea that each negative thought was having a compound effect on how I viewed myself and my life.

11.   The older and wiser me has learned to be very aware of my emotions and to check in with myself on several levels before allowing them to have the final say.

12.   Here are some of the lessons I've learned over the years to help me manage my emotions rather than allowing them to lead the way.

Validate your emotions first.

13.   When you find yourself riding the wave of emotion, it's important not to dismiss those feelings. Emotions can be a lot like unruly children in need of attention. Once we validate them, we allow them to be seen and have a voice.

14.   Feeling our emotions is an important part of life; it's what we do with them that can create problems.

15.   For example, if I'm feeling bored, sad, or lonely, I tend to turn to food for comfort. This usually doesn't end well. As I gain weight I then feel even worse because now my self-esteem suffers. Leaning into my emotions instead of numbing them with food has been a huge part of my process.

16.   When we validate our emotions, we become more aware and accepting of them, and we begin to understand where they come from. It's only in this place of awareness that we can see what power they may hold over us.

Be aware of your triggers.

17.   If you know you struggle with specific emotions, such as anger, jealousy, or fear, try to become aware of the circumstances that trigger them.

18.   In my own life, I have learned that I often feel angry when I am disrespected or unappreciated. So if I ask my kids several times to do something and they ignore me, I feel anger beginning to rise inside.

19.   Not too long ago I would have given in to the emotion and started to shout, whereas nowadays I'm able to tune in to the preceding thought—*they don't respect me*—recognize that it isn't true, and avert the anger.

Awareness is power; it gives us the control to choose how we respond.

20.   Always remember that emotion is derived from thought. If we find ourselves experiencing strong emotions, it's helpful to examine the thoughts that preceded them. Then ask the question, *are these thoughts based on truth, or my perception of the truth?*

Write it down.

21. One of the biggest tools in helping me deal with my emotions has been to write them down. I have been journaling daily for about three years now, always asking questions about my emotions and trying to dig beneath the surface-level thoughts.

22. If I feel at the mercy of my emotions, I'll ask a simple question in my journal, such as, *why do I feel so overwhelmed today?* From there I can work back through the sequence of events and thoughts that have led me there.

23. I will then ask a positive action question to engage with another emotion, such as, *what is one positive thing I can do for myself right now?*

24. If you don't have time to write, try to at least ask the questions.

Take responsibility.

25. How many times have you told someone that his or her actions made you feel a certain way? For example, "You made me angry when you were late."

26. It's true that other people's behavior and actions affect us all the time, but we also need to take responsibility for the emotions we feel in response to those words and actions. No one can make you feel anything; it's always your choice.

27.   So often the reactive emotions we feel are based on our own perception of the truth, and on the things that matter to us. Being late may be one of your triggers for anger, but for someone else it may be their norm and no big deal.

28.   Consider also that people act a certain way based on many influences that differ from your own, such as culture, upbringing, beliefs, and life experiences.

Take time away.

29.   When you're strongly connecting with a negative reactive emotion, it's important to take time away from the person or situation you are reacting to. Never act on strong emotion. Wait until you are feeling calm and have given yourself time to rationalize and think. Only then should you act.

30.   Even if the emotion is a positive one, it can still lead you down a destructive path. How many times have you done something you later regret in the name of love?

Create your mantra.

31.   It's easy to say, "Take time away," but hard to do in the heat of the moment. If I find myself beginning to anger and I'm not able or quick enough to remove myself from the situation, I

try to connect with my mantra. A mantra is just a word or short phrase that helps you become aware of your emotion and not be controlled by it.

32.   The word I use is "soft" because I associate this with a gentle temperament. For you it may be something completely different, depending on the emotion you are most reactive to.

33.   Ultimately it's important to remember that you are not your emotions—you have the ability to decide if they lead you or if you lead them.

34.   As you build awareness and learn to recognize your triggers, you will become increasingly savvy about when your emotions are serving you well and when you may need to take charge of them.

Here's another website I find particularly useful:

http://www.noovah.com/10-negative-emotions-their-messages-and-solutions/

For something a little more unusual you can take a look at this method of clearing negative emotions. Courtesy of Amy Bscher.

http://amybscher.com/emotional-freedom-technique-eft-meridian-tapping/

It's a good idea to educate us Auties on what facial expressions are telling us about emotions. You can do this by looking at pictures on line. I've put an example here.

Using the 1-5 gauge is a great visual tool to keep on display for your Auties to check themselves regularly and point out to themselves and you how they're feeling. This tools aims to help us understand where we are at any point and also to take action early to manage our emotions. To process our feelings so they doesn't build up into something bigger (meltdown, shutdown or freeze).

There is a lot of information about emotional management and ultimately improving your emotional intelligence. I've shared a few things here. I would recommend you explore free resources and information on this to help improve your Auties awareness of and what to do to assist processing that emotion positively. You, the support, may not be too good at this yourself so do this together. Let your Autie be the coach and help you to process your negative emotions to embed the process in themselves.

5 — **I can't stand this and ready to explode.** I want to hit someone, something, or throw something. I need an adult to help me go to a safe place so I can calm down.

4 — **I am getting too angry.** My brain isn't working clearly. I might say or do something I will be sorry for later. I need to go to my safe place to calm down.

3 — **I am getting really irritated.** I need to walk away from a bad situation. I will tell my teacher that I need a break.

2 — **I am doing OK.** I'm not pleased, but I'm not upset. I can stay where I am and keep working. I can control my anger by myself.

1 — **I am doing great.** I feel good about myself and about what is going on around me.

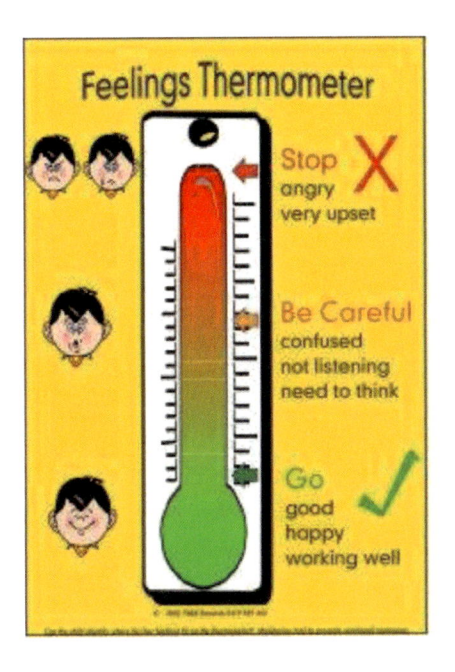

Goals and Aims

When I was in my late teens I had vague goals but I didn't have any confidence in myself or the slightest clue about organising myself to fulfil my dreams.

When I was 28 years old I went on a weekend programme which taught me about positivity; goals setting and visualisation. I can honesty tell you it changed my life, I felt like I had control and positivity about my future for the first time. I was overcoming a split with my first husband just after having our baby. I'm sure you'll agree it was a trying time. Up until then I'd worked hard to improve myself, but my anxiety was high and my ability to be optimistic about change and hope for bigger and better things was fairly limited. I learned a process (which I still use today) by Jack Black, Mindstore. He encouraged me, through his methodology, to look for the positive in life, to use positive language and to think big. I immediately started to positively and routinely practise this approach. From this approach I achieved the following and more:

- Met and married a wonderful, kind man

- Own and live in a beautiful home

- Had a successful career in Learning and Development

- Maintained my health and fitness

- Travelled around the world whilst being paid

- Developed a career in public speaking

- Identified myself as an Autie

- Had a wonderful second child (my first child is absolutely brilliant too, but I wasn't practising this technique then)

- Wrote this book.

The first step is to evaluate all areas of your life. Use Jack's "wheel of life" (below) to identify where you need to make changes. This may look very negative for your Autie when you start this process. They may feel each area of their life needs a lot of improvement.

In my first wheel analysis, wealth was somewhere I wanted to address as was my career. Through attending a Mindstore event and following the processes, I reached all my important goals fairly quickly.

The following tools are from the Jack Black, Mindstore processes I learnt. They are not Jack's process in it's entirety. I would recommend you attending a programme, it's life changing.

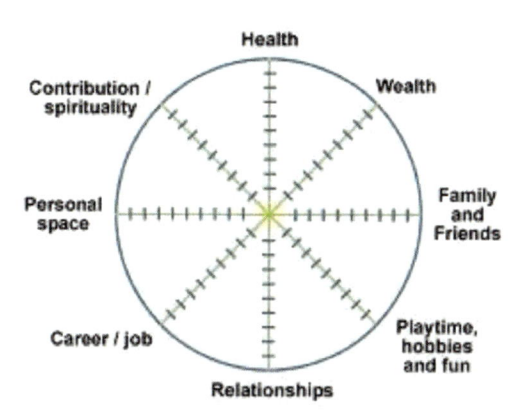

Simply give each area a score, the closer to the centre the lower the score, the closer to the perimeter the higher the score (the more satisfied you are with each area of your life). Here's an example (it's a fairly positive example), everyone's is individual and it's important you talk about what makes you score high, medium or low, what's your evidence and what kind of things do you want to do to improve your score. Remember to be honest, don't pretend things are better than they are. Also don't worry about the exact scores, really you're choosing high, medium or low.

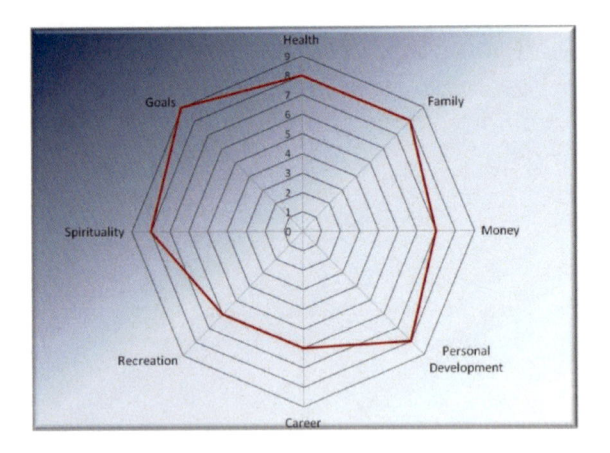

Big Goals

The process is then to go on to write out BIG and EXCITING goals. Write them as affirmations (as if they have already been achieved), for example:

"I am the training manager for a UK based blue chip company."

Or

"I earn £35,000 working in a local job I love with fantastic people."

Or

"I have many close and rewarding friendships in my life".

It's important to think about the way you write this goal. You can find many tools on-line to help you formulate these affirmations/goals for short term and long term goals. I wouldn't have more than seven goals you're working towards at once. In fact I usually have around five.

Positivity & Reframing

Remaining positive is an immensely important message here too. You MUST use positive language. As we Auties can lean towards negativity it's important to keep this in check. Language you use is a way of checking this: "I will do this"; "I'm great"; I'm getting very good at becoming positive" instead of negative or half-hearted language like: "I'm OK"; "I might do this"; "I'm rubbish at this". How we speak to ourselves and others is a key part to achieving our goals. This may seem trivial, but I can tell you it changed my life for the better.

You can find other resources to help you change your thinking from negative or neutral to positive.

Types of Language Examples		
Positive	Neutral	Negative
Yes	Might	No
I will	Maybe	I can't
Absolutely	Unsure	Never
Fantastic	So-so	Crap
I would like to feel better	OK	I feel terrible
I will find a solution	Might sort it	We're failing

The aim here is to only use positive language and to therefore avoid neutral and negative. Changing your language helps you to stay positive even when it's not the best situation. Thinking in a more solution based way rather than a negative way will help you achieve this.

Visualise your Success

Once you have written positive affirmations it's time to start thinking about your goals and therefore motivating yourself to achieve them. I found the best way to do this was through visualisation techniques and visual reminders of my goals. These are also very relaxing and soothing therefore very good as a counter to our high anxiety.

Again, I learnt these skills through Mindstore, McKenna Breen and Tony Robbins. I trained as a Neuro Linguistic Programming (NLP) practitioner so I could facilitate the practice for others. In my experience, most people found visualisation to be a very useful tool for a number of reasons: achievement, focus, anxiety management and relaxation. You can buy downloads to listen to for general goals like confidence or social skills. Remember us Auties struggle with motivation, therefore it's imperative that the person decides on their own goals. These don't have to be financial everyone has different expectations from life. If they are happy being confident and positive and not setting big goals, then little ones like travelling independently or buying their own clothes is enough.

http://www.mindstore.com

Controlling your moods

Due to our condition we can be very moody and grumpy. This isn't pleasant for our love ones or for us either. Teaching us to be positive will help us to look for the good and positive in a situation which will help us to regulate our moods. Also teaching relaxation techniques and receiving massage or healing or practising yoga may help.

State Management

The tool I have used for years is an NLP tool called "state management". It talks about states/moods being within our control. That we can get into a pattern of moods/states either positive or more likely negative. By changing our body position and energy we can choose more positive states/moods. It's fun to do. As a person living or working with an Autie, if you can practise positive, calm and fun states you'll find they rub off. Negativity will also rub off so it's an important practice for you too.

Using positive language (as mentioned earlier) will make a real difference to the quality of life, motivation and optimism of any person but as we're likely to be a negative group we need it countered with positive language and state. When you're communicating use words that are positive, upbeat and optimistic:

How are you? I'm absolutely wonderful today!

What's good about this?

You are amazing!

This isn't easy but you can do it!

The way you say it is important too. Us Auties tend to have monotone voices, so adding some intonation to increase excitement and interest is a good idea. They can learn to imitate this energy too when with people. The State Management Tool will help with this too.

Circles of Influence

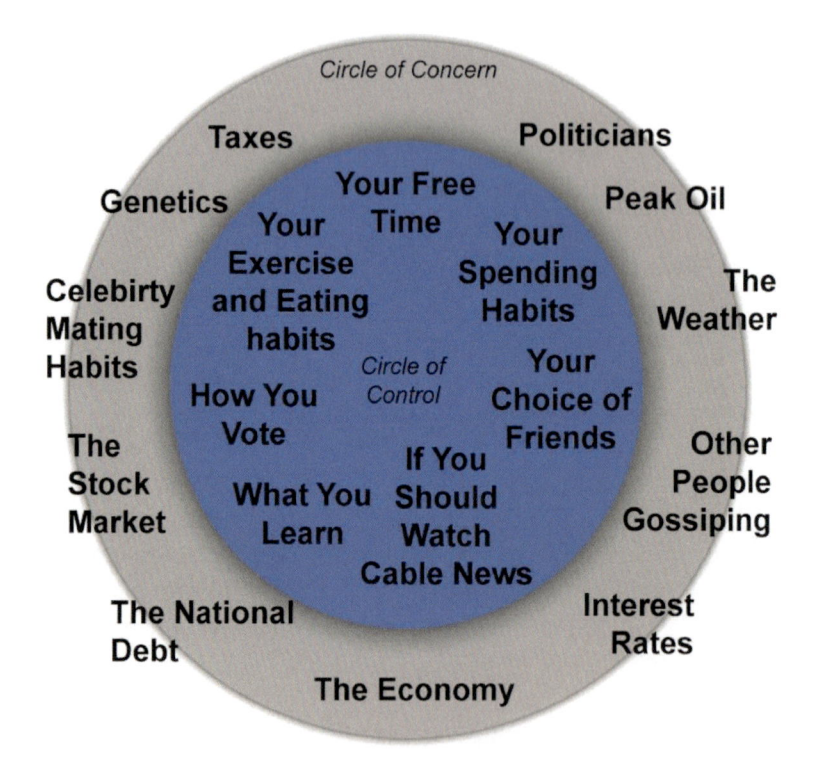

Circle of Concern

Taxes, Politicians, Genetics, Peak Oil, Celebirty Mating Habits, The Weather, The Stock Market, Other People Gossiping, The National Debt, Interest Rates, The Economy

Circle of Control

Your Free Time, Your Exercise and Eating habits, Your Spending Habits, How You Vote, Your Choice of Friends, If You Should Watch Cable News, What You Learn

Our anxiety can increase when we don't know how big a problem is in our lives and what to do about it. This tool was great for me as I used to worry about everything, Dracula, leprosy, oil supplies running out and many more things. When I was introduced to Stephen Covey's Circles of Control I let out a big sigh of relief. You'll see from the tool, it helps us to see what we can and can't influence and therefore concentrate on the right things in our lives.

You can use this to help us Auties get a good prospective of a situation or problem and see our role in it so we do take responsibility for our part but not everyone else's (a habit I personally had).

Opinion vs. Fact

I've noticed that many of us have an issue with the differences between facts and opinions. Consequently we can belief what people tell us as we see it as a fact rather than an opinion. This can get us into trouble and confuse us. However, more concerning, is that it can damage our self-esteem if we believe negative feedback without questioning it. I remember a former boss told me once that I was arrogant. As I knew the 3 step assertiveness model I used it by asking what she had noticed that made me seem arrogant (step 1 turned into a question). She replied with "it's not me that thinks that it's all the managers". Can you imagine how this would have affected my self-esteem if I didn't question its validity. I then asked why they thought this and she replied, "It's the way you walk." This was her trying to bully me. I instantly dismissed her comments and told her that the feedback was not valid and if the managers had an issue with the way I walk, that's their insecurity not mine.

Explain/Discuss what a fact is and what an opinion is. Ask them for facts and for opinions on their special interests.

You are aiming to ensure they are clear about the difference.

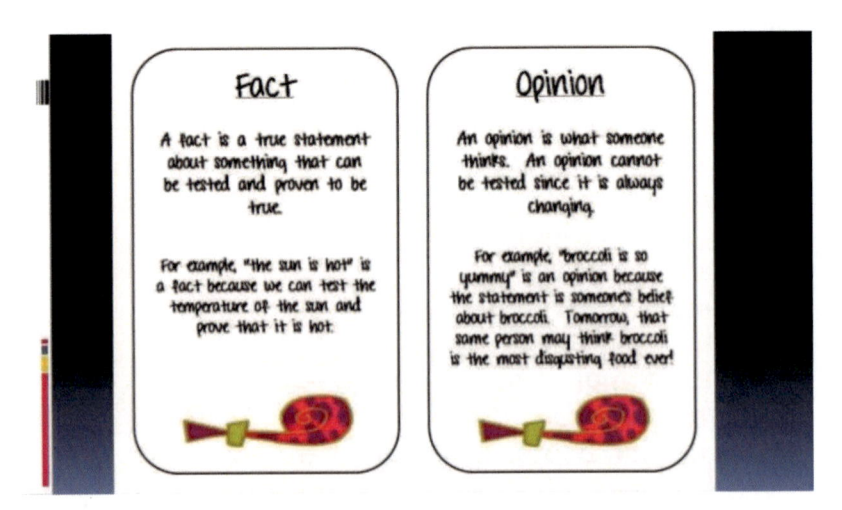

> **Fact**
>
> A fact is a true statement about something that can be tested and proven to be true.
>
> For example, "the sun is hot" is a fact because we can test the temperature of the sun and prove that it is hot.

> **Opinion**
>
> An opinion is what someone thinks. An opinion cannot be tested since it is always changing.
>
> For example, "broccoli is so yummy" is an opinion because the statement is someone's belief about broccoli. Tomorrow, that same person may think broccoli is the most disgusting food ever!

Inner Voice

Being your Autie's compassionate, supportive and positive coach is an important role, however, developing our own inner voice to be all those things is essential too. I speak to myself (outwardly) to self-motivate, encourage and calm myself whenever I need that. Regularly I hear myself saying, "Well done, you clever girl"; "that's OK, just give them a call and explain XYZ", "Just do this one thing and then you can look up the latest theory on…..". Speaking to ourselves with care is extremely important. This means the right tone of our voices as well as the right positive and encouraging words.

Practise this with your Autie.

How Self Management Skills and Social Sills are linked:

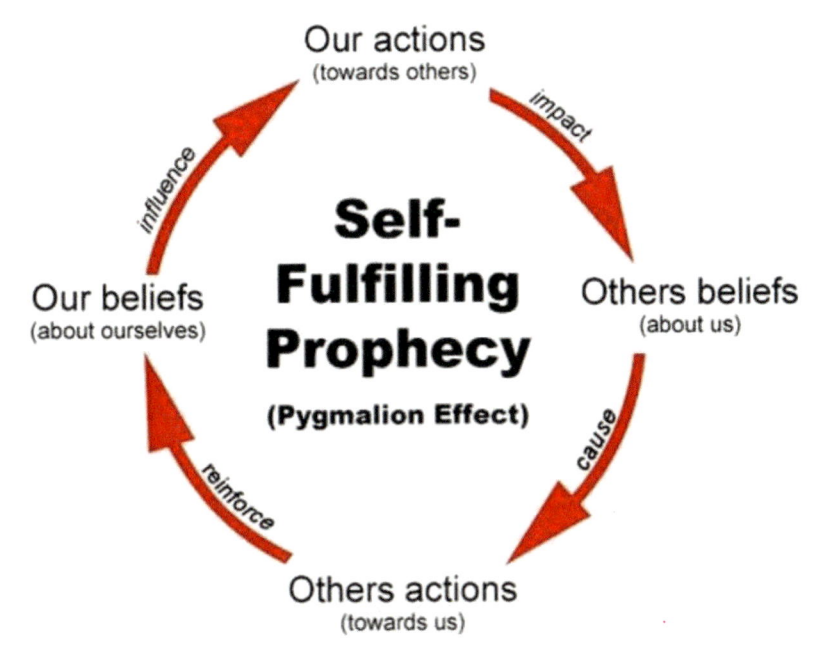

```
           Our actions
          (towards others)
    influence  ↑      ↘ impact

Our beliefs   Self-        Others beliefs
(about ourselves)  Fulfilling    (about us)
              Prophecy
           (Pygmalion Effect)

         ↖ reinforce    ↙ cause
           Others actions
            (towards us)
```

This model demonstrates how what we know, think and feel about ourselves determines how we behave which consequently determines how others respond to us and therefore feeds what we think and feel about ourselves. The previous sections, I hope, have encouraged positive thoughts and feelings about ourselves, however, we always have blind spots. Asking a person to give you feedback on your strengths and development needs is a great feedback mechanism, however, some feedback may not be relevant because of your Autistic brain. For example: Feedback that I'm unemotional would be unfair if it was because I was taking time to process my emotions or someone saying they thought I didn't have empathy because my face is less expressive (because of my Autism) could be damaging, we have to be careful here. We don't want to try to be an NT, but we want to learn some strategies to make us more aware of NTs and how they operate and modify when we want to for our own benefit, for more friendships for example. I want to stress however, NTs will need to do this too, otherwise it's exhausting for us Auties.

With that all said, I believe we (Auties and NTs) need to do work on ourselves before we can work on building relationships. This needs to be in the light of our Autism. I worked on improving myself for twenty plus years and was quite hard on myself for thinking like an Autie. Why didn't I need as many friendships as others and why did I not know how to hold on to them. With the lens of my Autism I can now understand myself and forgive myself, which ultimately effects self esteem. However, if I want friendships, I do need to learn what that looks like, how I can manage various situations to support both my friends' friendship needs and my own. I may have fewer friends than NTs; I may socialise on line more; I may not go to all the outings or only part of them. My close friends need to kind, understanding people. However if you want to get better a friendship management and skills the following paragraphs have some great information and resources.

Friendship Management

I, like most Auties, was totally confused by the friendship unspoken rules and therefore I gave up on making and maintaining friendships as I simply wasn't any good at it. I didn't know what to say and when. What were the right questions to ask at different points of the friendship without a rulebook it was all way too confusing and just led to more damage to my self-esteem. After meeting my second husband, who is a very competent socializer, I started to learn those rules. I still get it wrong sometimes but I have the fundamentals and my friends have to forgive me the rest and do, those who know about ASD anyhow.

Circles of friendship

One of the first things I needed to change was thinking about choosing my friends rather than them choosing me. Of course, it has to be both ways but I did tend to up end with friends or companions who wanted to be my friend rather than who I found interesting. Ensuring we know what makes a good friend for us is important, otherwise we can end up in a lot trouble as I did many times during my youth. Draw or write a list of the qualities of people you like:

adventurous	compassionate	exuberant	passionate
affable	conscientious	brave	patient
affectionate	considerate	fair-minded	persistent
agreeable	convivial	faithful	pioneering
ambitious	courageous	fearless	philosophical

amiable	courteous	forceful	placid
amicable	creative	frank	plucky
amusing	loving	friendly	polite
warm-hearted	decisive	funny	helpful
brave	determined	neat	honest
bright	diligent	generous	optimistic
broad-minded	diplomatic	gentle	rational
versatile	discreet	good	reliable
calm	dynamic	gregarious	reserved
careful	enthusiastic	energetic	resourceful
charming	easy-going	hard-working	romantic
kind	emotional	nice	willing
impartial	powerful	self-confident	witty
independent	practical	self-disciplined	unassuming
intellectual	pro-active	sensible	understanding

intelligent	loyal	sensitive	sympathetic
intuitive	quick-witted	shy	thoughtful
modest	quiet	sincere	tidy
inventive	straightforward	sociable	tough

Here's some examples above, this is not a full and comprehensive list just a starting place. Think about your friendships now, if you have any, and identify the personalities they have. Note that all the adjectives to describe them are not listed, so add your own.

For example: My husband is:

☐ warm

☐ kind

☐ modest

☐ messy

☐ reliable

☐ intelligent

☐ fun

☐ discreet

- polite

I have Autie friends who decide they want a boyfriend/girlfriend and then almost the first person that comes along they select. It's important to think about who you want to have in your life and don't settle for second best. Quality relationships are important to anyone, however, we Auties need positive role models to learn from and therefore creating this for us or ourselves is something to learn and put in place. You probably won't choose the same list for every friend. It's fun and educational to discuss the characteristics and how people demonstrate them so we can trust our judgement of others and potential friendship for the future.

For example: I know my husband is kind because he is very concerned if people are hurt physically or emotionally and tries to help them. He also has been very supportive to me when I haven't been well.

Creating and discussing evidence will help us to understand what we like about a person what we may have in common, what we can talk about and therefore what to do together.

Teaching us that people tell untruths and can be unkind is important otherwise we will be more vulnerable. Teaching us why they might do this is important too. Don't assume that we Auties will know this already. We may not understand why someone might be motivated to be behave in a cruel way because of jealousy; guilt; or because of their ego. I have encountered some cruel behaviours from both men and women, which I couldn't fathom. I've been told it could be because they are jealous of me because I'm prettier, cleverer and consequently more popular than them. This wouldn't have crossed my mind before as I can't imagine this. This may be because of my inability to guess other people's thoughts and feelings. I try to imagine what it would feel like to feel physically unattractive and overweight, to look at someone I think is attractive and feel jealously, but I honesty never do. I like looking at attractive faces as they are like a work of art to me, not something to be jealous of.

Once we have started to gain a clearer picture about what characteristics we appreciate in a friend you can also share information about levels of friendship. This will demonstrate that just because we have met someone it doesn't automatically make them a friend. I remember searching for books on friendship as I was looking for something to explain the complexities. I came across this way of looking a friendships vs. acquaintances.

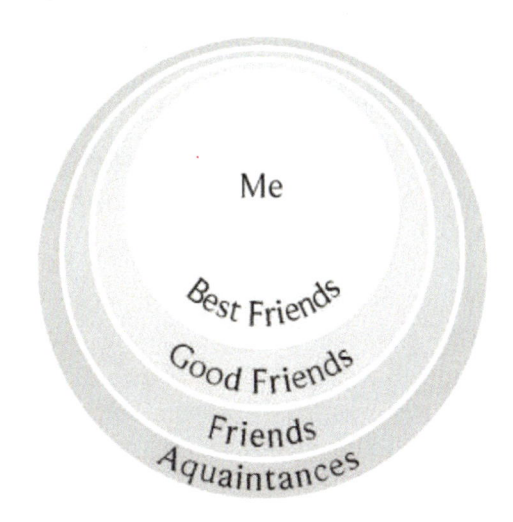

Me
Best Friends
Good Friends
Friends
Aquaintances

Showing the differences in levels of friendships. Who would populate each area and why. It doesn't matter so much about the number of people in each level as long as your Autie is fulfilled socially. Ask if they think they have enough friends and what they like about their friendship circle. You can use this lesson I found on the internet on yourself or your Autie.

Extract from: Circles of Friendships

>A Lesson Plan from Life Planning Education: A Youth Development Program (Chapter Four)
>
>Purpose: To recognise different kinds of friends.
>
>Materials: For each participant, one copy of the handout, Circles of Friendships; newsprint and markers or board and chalk; pens/pencils
>
>Time: 20-30 minutes
>
>Planning Notes:
>
>For Step 3, draw a large illustration of your circles of friends on newsprint or the board. To do so, follow the instructions in Step 4.
>
>Procedure:
>
>Point out that not all friends are best friends or even close friends. In fact, friends can range from very close to not so close. Ask if participants know what you mean.

Display the large illustration of your circles of friendships. Explain that this represents your friendships, with your closest friends in the circle closest to the centre, casual friends in the next circle, and acquaintances in the outside circle.

Distribute the handout and ask participants to make their own friendship circles:

Write your name in the centre circle.

Write the name(s) of your closest friend(s) in the next circle.

Write in the middle circle the names of casual friends, those you know well enough to talk to or have lunch with, but not as well as your closest friends.

Write in the outer circle the names of acquaintances, people you speak with sometimes, but do not think of as friends.

Allow five to ten minutes for participants to complete their circles.

Conclude the activity using the discussion points below.

Discussion Points:

Some people have many several best friends while others have one best friend. Some have many casual friends while others think of most people as acquaintances. What did you learn about your own friendships from this activity?

How did you decide who is in your inner circle? The middle circle? The outside circle?

What are the ages of your closest friends? Casual friends? Acquaintances? Why do people choose friends of different ages? Are there advantages from having an older adolescent or adult as a friend? Disadvantages?

In which circles did you place friends of the same? Other sex? Why?

What are two things that you would talk about with close friends, but not with casual friends or acquaintances? Why?

Would you like to make changes in your friendship circles? Which ones?

What three things you could do to get to know an acquaintance better? To grow closer to a casual friend?

Life Planning Education, Advocates for Youth, Updated 2009.

Adapted with permission from Sexuality Education: A Curriculum for Adolescents, ETR Associates, Santa Cruz, CA, 1984. For information about this and other related materials, call 1-800-321-1407.

See appendix for a full exercise on building friendships in groups.

Plan Friendship Time

As we can either over contact our friends or the total opposite: "out of sight and out of mind", it's a good idea for the person to project manage their friendships. By thinking about their friendships and planning regular activities with them and putting some time in their diary on a weekly or monthly basis to plan their friendship time and time to plan activities with your friends. For example: a cinema date or theatre if you don't have a regular activity already planned. Remembered knowing the start and finish times is key as is doing a structured activity. Friendships through special interests is another opportunity, regular dog walks, cinema or theatre trips or motor shows. This can be more challenging when we're younger as we're not in charge of our own diaries and or may not know about these opportunities to build friendships, therefore our family, advocates, friends can help us start these activities.

Staying Safe - identifying dangers in relationships

Some of things to look out for:

Bullies

People who are cruel and abusive to you because they feel insecure about themselves. They also want to bully others to gain credibility with others.

Users

People who want to use you for their own gain. They may appear friendly but manipulate you to do things for their benefit. Wolf in sheep's clothing.

Bad influencers

People who have low standards in life who may be self-destructive and encourage you to join them. They may encourage you into vices like casual sex, drugs and alcohol.

You'll need to teach your Autie that people are not always what they seem. People lie and you need to learn to watch out for these people in our lives.

We may be susceptible to drugs and alcohol as part of a self-management strategy to reduce our anxiety. This only makes things worse as it would for a NT. Therefore, teaching Auties about drugs, alcohol, sexual relationships factually is essential.

The main reason I partook in vices was to manage my anxiety and to fit-in and have friends. If we have positive, trusting relationships with role models (these can be family or friends or teachers etc.) and we know about the grey we can avoid these dangers.

Social Skills

There are great resources out there but sometimes it's as confusing as to which skills to focus on. Here's an extract from the NAS website which has some great advice:

Social skills: important things to remember

Here are some additional ideas and things to remember to help you when dealing with social situations. This does not cover every possible situation you may find yourself in, but it does provide advice for some of the most common circumstances:

1. Rules change depending on the situation and person you are speaking to. For example, it would be appropriate to say 'Hiya' to a friend but 'Hello' to your boss. A good example of this is the story of a man who was told that it was polite to go up to people and smile and shake their hand when he met them. This was appropriate most of the time. However, when he attended a family member's funeral people thought he was being insensitive because he was walking around with a big smile when they were feeling sad.

2. If you make a mistake and upset someone it does not mean they do not like you. Usually, saying sorry helps. If you are not sure what you have done to upset someone, ask.

3. Sometimes it is ok not to tell the truth to make someone else happy (e.g. saying they do not look fat, even if they do). Some people call these 'little white lies'. Try thinking of some situations where this may be the case with a family member or key worker.

4. Saying 'please' and 'thank you' is appropriate in all situations. This shows other people that you are a polite person.

5. Even if you do not want to socialise with other people and prefer to be on your own, it is a good idea to develop your social skills. In particular, the links below to advice about having a conversation may be useful. These will help you to act in an appropriate way when you are in a social situation that you cannot avoid, e.g. a family party. Again, this will show other people that you are a polite person.

Above extract is courtesy of the National Autistic Society's website:

http://www.autism.org.uk/about/communication/social-skills.aspx

I agree that learning social skills mainly through my career has helped me to function in the NT world. So let's have a look at some more things to help yourself/you Autie.

Self-Awareness

We looked at some tools earlier in this chapter to help us know ourselves. This is about awareness of how we interact in social situations. I find knowing our condition helps us here. Continue to read information about ASD so you know the typical challenges we face. Looking at photos and video footage of yourself would be another way to do this. It's important that we don't expect to change who we are here as we need to be ourselves but we can learn some techniques that may help just by having more awareness of ourselves. A caveat I would add though is that we want to investigate with interest and curiosity not with a critical and negative voice.

Making Conversation in pairs or groups

One of my observations of myself, my children and my clients is that we all feel extremely self-conscience when we're noticed. It feels like we're on stage performing and we've forgotten our lines and the top theatre critics are writing their reviews then and there! I think because we can see and feel so much that's going on we think others are picking up the same as us, which they're not and we also struggle with verbal communication. The key is to relax into interactions (state management) and understand that other people are really usually thinking about themselves. The more I think about ensuring the other person is comfortable by smiling and welcoming them the easier it is for me.

I've already shared the some tools to help you feel relaxed but studying what charming looks like as a role model is very good tip. If you take Alexander Armstrong from Pointless for example. You can see how relaxed, fun, polite and encouraging he is. He appears at ease which in turn makes the people they are interacting with feel relaxed. State Management tool will help you achieve this too. How about practising the state of "confidence". Visualising yourself confident in a future event is another way to develop your social skills.

Rapport Building

Rapport building is an NLP tool also known as "matching and mirroring". It suggests that people build relationships by going through different levels of information sharing:

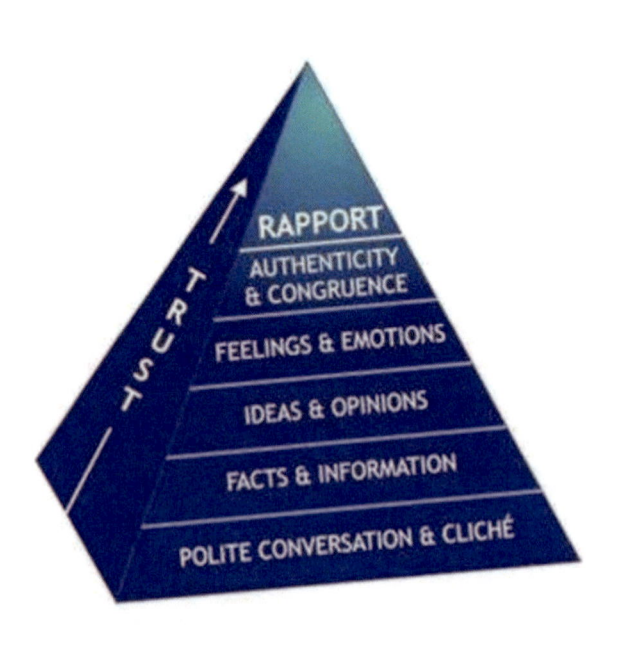

Model copyright to 'The Rapport Builder' website

This model suggests we start at the bottom and work our way up. I believe that we Auties regularly would share our feelings and emotions or quite personal facts about ourselves upon first meetings or to strangers. We don't seem to know this approach that NTs tend to use. It does seem very unnecessary and time wasting however it's helpful for us to be aware of it so we interact with more people successfully. Here's some examples of each level:

Polite conversation/cliché: Good morning or smiling

Facts and Information: Sharing things like your name or where you live; if you are married or have children.

Ideas and Opinions: What you think of something in the news or another person. For example: You think Hilary Clinton may win the USA election. I'd like the Rail Companies to improve their services.

Feelings and Emotions: Sharing feelings and emotions will be the most intimate thing you can share. Sharing how something makes you feel or how you feel about that person brings you to the top of the triangle.

Here's another online resource that explains the tool very well:

http://www.therapportbuilder.com/default.aspx?cid=32

The RAPPORT PYRAMID™ - COMMUNICATION SEQUENCE:

There are common stages and often a specific sequence of communication that people go through in order to get to that 'place of rapport'. For some it is intuitive, and they may or may not go through all of the stages to arrive at rapport. For others it is hard work, and they may have difficulty going beyond polite conversation.

Stage # 1 – Polite conversation & cliché…

Something the English are very good at, the main topic being the weather. It sometimes doesn't even involve eye contact or listening, often expressed via the mouth without troubling the brain. Topics are 'safe' and often concluded with a cliché e.g. *'all's fair in love and war'*. Rapport at this stage is far off.

Stage # 2 – Facts & Information...
This usually employs some degree of listening and thought process but tends to involve 'reporting' rather than 'communicating'. They can be delivered quite dispassionately, often via a series of statements with little need to involve personal conviction. Rapport is still far off, however we are beginning to reveal the building blocks of what may be important to us.

Stage # 3 – Ideas & Opinions...
Now we are definitely engaging our brain, we are 'surfing our mind' and then transmitting what we think may be appropriate to the issue in hand. We are now revealing where we are coming from by submitting our opinions, (positive or negative), agreement or disagreement. Dependent upon the manner in which we do this we may well have opened the door for rapport to come right in.

Stage # 4 – Feelings & Emotions...
Now we are involving our 'soul' which is our **'Thinker', 'Chooser' & 'Feeler'**. By expressing how we feel and displaying our emotions via the words we use, our tone of voice, our body language and pace, we are signaling: *"this is how I really feel; these are the choices I have made. I am listening and responding to what you say (although my perception may be something*

different and I am reacting rather than responding)." If this matches the depth of your feeling we are connecting at a deeper level then the door is even wider open for rapport to occur.

Stage # 5 – Congruence…
I am now being myself, not who I think everyone else thinks I should be. I am comfortable and at peace through being myself. I am displaying honesty and sincerity because I am being authentic. Although I may adapt my behaviour to improve communication, I am doing and being what I said I would do and be: there is congruency in my words and behaviours; the message is you can trust me. We are almost at rapport.

Stage # 6 – Rapport
We have a close and harmonious connection, there is mutual understanding and I sense empathy. There is an affinity and I am therefore prepared to trust you. We have **RAPPORT.**

Speaking

Speaking can be hard for us Auties for a few reasons.

- We feel so self-conscience

- Our voices feel/sound too loud or weird

- We don't know what we think or feel in a situation so don't know how to respond

- We don't know what to say in certain situations, we're not experienced enough or don't have the social rules

- We have low self-esteem and confidence in our social skills so give up

- We feel disassociated with the world, we're different

- We find it hard to put words together

- Are social energy is so low we just don't have anything left to give

Therefore learning lots of the models we've already covered will help with many of these situations such as: managing our social energy; positivity etc. However, there will be some skills we'll need to learn on top of these.

We need to learn:

- What does a good conversation look and sound like?

- What are some good conversation starters?

- How long should I stay talking to this person?

- How to mix in the group.

- What are appropriate things to share and at what times and what are not? (Rapport tool and NAS extract)

We Auties learn social skills like a subject at school so give us the time and support to this. There are many resources designed to help us do this already. This is a particularly good activity:

http://do2learn.com/organizationtools/SocialSkillsToolbox/ParticipatingWithOthers.htm

Overall however, I think we need good role models who will trust and who will help us learn these strategies with love and encouragement.

Here's one you could start with from Joel Shaul's website who helps us learn that conversations are about taking turns and linking what we say. You can use the pictures of the chain links to show successful conversations and then the broken ones to show when a person says something to break the chain. Of course when we first learn the skill it will be stilted so be prepared for it to improve gradually.

Explain and practise conversation here by explaining when we take it in turns to speak we do this taking turns and talking about linked subjects or information. If we suddenly start talking about something totally unconnected we break the chain.

Breaking the Chain will seem odd and confusing. As we are (usually) very visual learners we'll benefit from using these pictures as feedback or prompts when practising.

The Conversation Box This activity is to help young people with ASD to select valid and reciprocal forms of conversation instead of monologues and lectures. 1. Print and cut out the eight cards. I suggest you print out three sets so it creates a decent sized deck. You can put them in a box like this one: 2. Print out the illustrated panels as teaching aids and as references when you are doing the activity. Here is a link to a longer explanation, as well as all of the downloads:

http://autismteachingstrategies.com/autism-strategies/the-conversationbox-conversation-training-tool-for-children-with-high-functioning-autismand-aspergers/

Joel has asked me to mention that some the activities on his site are derived from a method described in:

Relationship Development Intervention with Children, Adolescents and Adults, Steven Gutstein and Rachelle Sheely, 2006, Anthenaeum Press.

Here's some example questions that can be used in social situation you can practise with your Autie:

Making plans together

Sharing feelings together

Remembering things together

Comparing interests

Comparing what you think

Figuring something out together

Making something funny together

Making plans together "How about if we…" "Do you think we could…" "Hey, let's…" "Do you want to…" "What are you doing later?" autismteachingstrategies.com

Sharing feelings together "That makes me feel _____. How does that make YOU feel?" "I'm worried. What about you?" "I will be so happy when _____. How about you?" "Are you feeling _____? Me too."

Comparing interests "I'm interested in _____. Are you?" "I like _____. How about you?" "I can't stand _____. What about you? "_____ is bad. What do you think?" autismteachingstrategies.com

Remembering things together "Do you remember that time when…?" "Remember when you and I…?" "I was thinking about back when our whole class…" "I can remember when we _____. Do you?" autismteachingstrategies.com

Comparing what you think "I think that _____. What do you think?" "My family believes _____. How about yours?" "I see your point." "I agree." "I disagree." autismteachingstrategies.com Figuring something out together "How should we…" "Can I help you to…" "Can you help me to…" "Let's try together to…" "What should I do?" autismteachingstrategies.com

Creating fantasies together [Example: "What would you think if soda came out of the drinking fountain?"] "Wouldn't it be great if…" "Wouldn't it be crazy if…" autismteachingstrategies.com

Making something funny together "Do you want to hear something funny?" "What you just said cracked me up!" "Did you hear the joke about…" "I saw something funny. Do you want to see it?".

You can use these examples to help practise conversation using the chain.

As already mentioned, the NAS has some great material on their website, here's some more useful guidance:

Extract from the NAS Website

How can I end a conversation?

Watch out for signals that someone wants to end a conversation with you. These may include:

o not asking questions back

o looking around the room

o yawning

o saying they have something else to do

Do not get upset if a person does this. Sometimes it is better to end a conversation before you run out of things to say.

If you want to end the conversation, say something like, "Well I'd better be going now" before saying "Goodbye" because it is more polite than just saying "Goodbye" and walking away. Try to think of some other ways to end a conversation.

Face reading

http://www.educateautism.com/free-materials-and-downloads.html/category/emotions.html

I think this is linked with the knowing your emotions section. You can buy cards or find resources on line with facial expressions to help us learn what these expressions mean. I still am not always sure as many faces look angry to me. I know I have trouble reading this "so having a script to ask the person how they're feeling works well, especially if they are friends.

Say something like: "You look upset (this covers anger, fear, and confusion) is there something wrong/bothering you. This show's you've noticed something and that you care (we often care too much).

Then you can give the space to tell you or say "No, I'm OK". Sometimes NTs will say "No" but there is something wrong. By sharing with your close friends that you find it difficult reading their emotions accurately you'll encourage them to explain more directly. If they don't want to, respect that they don't want to talk to you about this subject; that's OK. If they are rude to you because you don't understand then it could be because they are upset over a situation (you don't know about) so give them some slack - they're emotional. However, if they are just being rude and you've noticed this behaviour before, it's probably not a positive friendship for you so it's worth thinking about what's in this relationship for you. You don't need to tell them this at that moment or at all. Remember the OK Corral tool and the assertive behaviours.

Facial expressions

I thought I was good at reading faces and I think I may even be too good, but this can be too much information and confusing when there's lots of other stuff going on, the sensory stuff. Eye contact can feel very intrusive so I now accept I can't read it well and aim to read what I can but don't get to bogged down with it. I focus on the state management tool, being friendly and confident and then take in the information I can from voice tone, words and body language. If there's a lot of people to do this with all at once it can be challenging and tiring so I allow for this but planning my social communications as much as I can and then taking time to refuel (social energy). Remember this is easier to do as an adult so give your Autie kids a break and yourself if you're Autie. Not expecting quite so much from myself actually has lead to a better quality of social engagement.

Cambridge University Autism Research Centre has developed a CD-ROM programme called *Mind Reading*. It was developed to help people with an ASD to recognise the emotion that someone is feeling using their facial expression. The *Mind Reading* CD-ROM has been very successful and researchers at the University hope to be able to make a device that tells people with an ASD what emotion another person is feeling using a small camera and computer in the future. However, research into this is in the very early stages and so it will be a while before this is available.

Eye Contact - only if right for your person

The jury is out on this issue. My own experience of eye contact is that it improved for me as I got older, but it still feels uncomfortable with certain people and in intense situations. It's like I'm seeing into the other person's soul. It's not always a nice place!

I do think it's important if we are going to be going into mainstream school and the workplace to aim to develop this, however, it should never be done under duress. It should be the Autie's own decision to develop this if they wish, as with all of these tools.

One Autism Treatment Specialist from Toronto, Canada supports the idea that eye contact should "feel good" for children and adults on the spectrum. Whereas some behaviour therapy programs physically manipulate ("prompt") students to face the teacher and some use food reinforcement to elicit short and likely uncomfortable glimpses, Jonathan Alderson, founder of the Integrative Multi-Treatment Intervention (IMTI) Program takes a uniquely different approach. He trains parents and therapist to express acceptance and love through their gaze as a way to help make eye contact less intrusive and more inviting. Here is a reprint of Mr. Alderson's blog post on eye contact:

Eye Contact Should Feel Good for Kids with Autism
by J Alderson on June 22, 2011

This morning during a training session with therapists, I led a discussion about the nuances of teaching "eye contact" to our Autie student. We came to three important conclusions:

1) Eye contact should not be so narrowly defined as only eye-to-eye contact.

Instead, children with autism should be encouraged to look at and to watch a person's entire face including their mouth, eye brows, nose and other facial features.

In many therapies, students are expected to look directly into therapists' eyes on command: "Look at me. Look." A child who looks up at their face but not exactly into the therapist's eyes will not be praised and will often be physically guided to do so. The problem with this narrow perspective is that it is not necessarily natural, even for typically developing toddlers. Especially for children 0-3 years old, while they most definitely seek and track other's eyes, and especially those of his parents, they also spend a good amount of time studying other facial features. Importantly, toddlers and infants learn about communication and language production by watching mouths, eye brows and hand gestures all of which provide information about the nuances of the dialogue. Speech and language pathologists will confirm that a good portion of language is learned by watching and imitating mouth movements. By limiting or forcing a child with autism to look only directly at eyes, we are limiting/ inhibiting/ slowing down their communication learning and language acquisition.

2) Eye contact should not be forced or physically manipulated

Instead, you should make a positive association between eye contact and having autonomy/ control along with a positive relational experience.

When a therapist holds a child's chin turning his head to make the child look at her, the child loses his autonomy. He is controlled rather than being in (his own) control. He may have a negative experience, having his chin moved against his will, that becomes associated with making eye contact. The next time eye contact is requested, the negative associations of losing control and being physically forced may be triggered. This is behavioural science 101. Avoidance is sure to follow.

When a therapist withholds an item that a student wants, perhaps up by his eyes, to force the student to look then eye contact has been 'manipulated." Getting what is wanted is made conditional on looking at the therapist. The child learns that giving what is wanted to someone else can be used as leverage to get something you yourself want. (Giving freely as a kindness and courtesy is not a part of this system unfortunately.) Since making eye contact and observing others is a behaviour/a habit that can be extremely beneficial for a student to learn by, it is in the therapists' and students best interest to encourage children with autism to enjoy looking at others simply out of curiosity and interest – observing just to watch, to see what is happening, to understand…not only when an adult is forcing or manipulating them to do so.

3) Eye contact should not only be associated with demands and reprimands.

Instead, a child should experience as many occasions as possible of looking at another person's eyes and face and feeling loved, accepted and praised.

Like a teenager walking into the house after school who avoids contact with his parents' eyes knowing if he looks at them they'll ask him about the chores he hasn't done, children with autism learn early on that eye contact with an adult is associated with a demand. "Look at me so I can ask you to do something." I have observed dozens of therapy sessions where eye contact between the child and therapist is only ever associated with either a demand or with the child being reprimanded and judged. "Look at me when I'm talking to you! Don't do that again!" Given this association, it is easy to understand why the students don't generalize looking more often at others outside of therapy sessions.

Of course we want a child's attention when we are talking about important and serious stuff. But we should equally engage eye contact and observation behaviour when we are communicating affection, praise, positive affirmations, and love. Ask your child or student with autism to look at you and immediately smile. Don't make a request or demand of them to smile back or to answer a question. Just let them see you smiling. Invite them to look a little bit longer than usual. Allow them time to become interested in your smile, your lips, teeth, and eyes. If they do look for longer than usual, praise them for their interest. Again, don't make a demand, simply celebrate and acknowledge the eye contact that you received. Do this over and over many times a day. This will establish many positive associations between eye contact and other people's faces.

My son finds eye contact more challenging than my daughter who's ten years younger. It's very individual. He does want to improve these skills so we're now working on improving his eye contact knowledge and skills. There has to be times however when he doesn't need to practise eye contact, when he can avoid it if he wishes. I do want to stress however, we are working to help the NT world to understand us Auties and that means compromise on their part. The more they know about us the more flexible they can be, this is still something that needs to improve in society.

Jonathan's book *challenging the Myths of Autism* debunks common negative stereotypes about people with ASD and is a good resource for parents and professionals who want to learn to reframe common stereotypes into more humane and more hopeful understandings about autism.

I use eye contact lightly and remind myself that NTs don't focus as intently as us and therefore won't be noticing as much as us Auties. This helps me not to feel as self-conscious as I did when I was younger. Reminding myself that most people are thinking about how they are communicating and therefore are not so scrutinizingly focusing on me helps a lot.

Listening

I was reminded the other day when I met a HR Director of the importance of listening. She bombarded me with questions but didn't give me the time to answer before her next question was fired. I was very tempted to tell her she needed to improve her listening skills. She was an NT.

We've got a lot going on so listening can be a real challenge. When I listen I really listen but this takes oodles of concentration and therefore depletes my social energy levels. As a learning and development professional and teacher I really must be able to listen to do my job however sensory issues, anxiety, my drive for my own agenda (special interest) and challenges reading messages have meant it requires me to choose to focus. Like all of the social skills it requires practice. There are some visual prompts below to demonstrate what constitutes good listening:

To listen well, *hear all the words.*	To listen well, *ask and find out more.*
To listen well, *turn off other thoughts.*	To listen well, *look towards the person.*

Questions

When we looked at the assertiveness model we could see PUSH (inform/tell) and PULL (question and listen). Therefore to be able to be assertive we need the ability to do all of these things. In my experience most people spend too much time "telling" everyone what they're thoughts and feelings are and not enough asking questions or listening. Some of us Auties can do this very well, especially when talking about our special interest. Conversely however we can say nothing and just look blank. In this case we are like a "wet rag", this can lead to many problems: extreme meltdowns at home; being a target for bullies; and low self-esteem. Finding our voice will come with the other exercises as sometimes we don't know what we think and feel. Be patient here. Knowing all these tools and about our own ASD will help us immensely.

Waiting

This has always been a problem for me, although I was so timid as a child and young adult I always waited till last whilst inside I was screaming with impatience, very stressful. I know this is a weakness for me but I have learnt to use self-talk to help me here by reassuring myself that I will get a turn. Practising turn-taking and rewarding patience with praise will encourage this behaviour. Strategies whilst waiting is something my husband taught me too. I always bring a book or some work to do to keep myself occupied and distracted. Particularly practise the 3 step feedback tool and role-play testing situations.

Sharing

I don't like sharing, neither does my son. Knowing that if we share it will come back to us is a good positive message. Sometimes we just don't want to share, if it's reasonable I allow this as my parents used to allow my sister to take my clothes anytime she wanted and I felt this was very unfair, I'd bought these clothes they belonged to me I should be able to decide if I wanted to share them or not. However, if it's unreasonable then I would encourage sharing as a good characteristic. Here's some examples you could use of times it's good to share and times it's not:

Reasonable to Share	Unreasonable
If you have sweets and your friend doesn't	If it's particularly special to you (valuable in some way)
If your friend lends you things it's good to reciprocate	If it was a special gift from someone
If you're finished with something and have no need for it it's good to give it to someone else	If it costs a lot of money
If they are a guest	If it means you will suffer by sharing
If it's communal	If the person refuses to share with you
If it doesn't belong to you	If the person is irresponsible with your property

Seeing Things from Other's Perspectives

Another Neuro-Linguistic Programming (NLP) tool I use is 3rd Position Tool. This enables the person using it to see things from other's points of view or a least to try to. It's a physical movement tool too, this makes it fun to use.

If you have a conflict with someone, this happens in life, you can use this three stage tool to see the situation more clearly by seeing it from three different points of view. Here's an explanation of how do this:

By **Kate Burton**

Part of Coaching with NLP For Dummies Cheat Sheet (UK Edition)

Perceptual positions help you imagine what difficult situations look like when viewed with others' eyes. The term refers to the ability to imagine what others perceive by imagining that you are that other person. In NLP this links with the assumption that 'the map is not the territory' and offers a way to enrich an individual's map of the world.

- First position is your natural perspective, where you're fully aware of what you think and feel regardless of those around you. This is the place that clients find most familiar. They've come to coaching because they already have an awareness of their own perspective and the problems they face.

- Second position is about imagining what it's like to be another person. Some people are very good at considering others' needs and concerns; for a more self-focused client, imagining second position is a completely alien notion.

- Third position is an independent position where you act as a detached observer noticing what's happening in the relationship between two other people. Good coaches naturally step into this impartial role. In coaching, encourage the client to take this position in order to gain an impartial insight into a situation, particularly to view a relationship the client has with another person.

You can introduce perceptual positions to clients by having them physically move to different chairs or places in a room as you describe and discuss the three positions, asking them to notice what they experience while standing or sitting in each position. The real learning comes by stepping out of first position to explore second and third positions and see what light it sheds on a situation.

Trying New Things

Learning about comfort zones was a great way to look at change in a positive way.

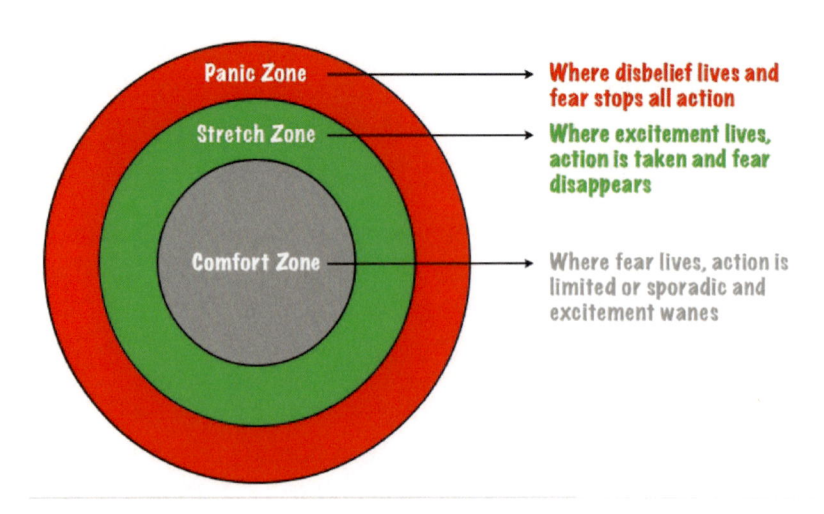

Panic Zone	Where disbelief lives and fear stops all action
Stretch Zone	Where excitement lives, action is taken and fear disappears
Comfort Zone	Where fear lives, action is limited or sporadic and excitement wanes

If we never grow our comfort zones we will lead more limiting lives and therefore encouraging courage to try something new and broaden our horizons, as long as it's safe, will have a beneficial influence on the quality of our lives. When I travelled for work, although I was frightened, I learned so much and grew in confidence. I am not suggesting that this has to be the comfort zone stretch for your Autie, but I have found this to be a positive approach in my life.

Explain that everyone has a comfort zone where we follow our usual habits. Explain that it's important to see stretch as growth. This might be trying a new food or paying for the items at the supermarket or applying for a job or traveling around the world. Explain that we all feel scared at this time but we enjoy the rewards of stretching our comfort zones.

If we don't create planned and supported change this can easily push us into the panic zone so having some communication and strategies to identify if this is happening at any point is essential to ensure the person doesn't shy away from change and in effect shrinks their comfort zone.

I pushed myself too hard throughout my life and paid the price of burnout. However I still want to stretch myself. The difference now is that I listen to myself and use more coping strategies.

As with all these tools, you can find more by typing the tool into the search engine.

Other resources to download Grey Thinking:

Thanks to all the links providers I've used in my book. I recommend readers research more as they feel would benefit them. You can also find more information about tools that can help you improve this skills and behaviours here:

https://www.do2learn.com/

http://autismteachingstrategies.com/free-social-skills-downloads-2/

https://www.mnsu.edu/comdis/kuster4/part103.html

http://modelmekids.com/social-skills-lesson-plans.html

https://www.autismspeaks.org/sites/default/files/documents/family-services/improve_social.pdf

http://www.positiveaboutautism.co.uk/page31/page31.html

Competencies Checklist -

Please use the list below to plan, monitor and record your Autie's progress on the following behaviours as you work your way through the book. This learning journey may take months or years, that's OK, I'm still working on my "Grey Thinking".

Skill/Behaviour	Resource /page	Completed date
I can say no politely	Chapter 6, Assertiveness & Saying "No"	
I can tell people what I think and/or how I feel appropriately and assertively	Chapter 6, Assertiveness & Emotions	
I can read my own emotions and respond positively to them	Chapter 6 Assertiveness, Emotions, Listening, Speaking	
I can use positive language and reframe negatives	Chapter 6, Positive Language & Reframing	
I can take control of my mood through state management and a positive inner voice	Chapter 6, State Management, Inner Voice, Positivity, Reframing	

Skill/Behaviour	Resource /page	Completed date
I can organise my time, through planning and sticking to my plan	Chapter 4, Triggers Chapter 6, Time Management & Assertiveness	
I know who I am and my characteristics	Chapter 6, Know Yourself and Self Awareness 3 Step Feedback – Asking others for feedback 3rd Position	
I value myself and trust myself	Chapter 5, Happiness Chapter 6 Inner Voice Positivity Know myself	
I can judge appropriate conversation subjects to situations	Chapter 6, Social Skills Section	
I know a varied selection of conversation starters	Chapter 6, Social Skills Section	
I can review my friendships and decide on how and when I'd like to socialise with them	Chapter 6, Social Skills Section	
I can project manage my friendships	Chapter 6, Time Management& Social Skills Section	

Skill/Behaviour	Resource /page	Completed date
I can identify my anxiety triggers and minimise them	Chapter 4	
I participate in healthy special interests in balance with my responsibilities	Chapter 5	
I can manage my social energy levels	Chapter 4	
I can review my happiness levels and set life goals to remedy any deficits	Chapter 5 Chapter 6, Wheel of life and Goal setting	
I have a anxiety survival pack for emergencies	Chapter 4	
I am aware of social cues	Chapter 6, Social Skills Section	
I can read common body language	Chapter 6, Social Skills, Rapport and Recognising Emotions facial expressions	
I can identify negative thinking and language in myself and change it	Chapter 6, Negativity, Reframing, Positive Language	
I can see the difference between opinion and fact	Chapter 6, Facts and Opinions	

Skill/Behaviour	Resource /page	Completed date
I can see the difference between big and small decisions and their potential consequences	Chapter 6, Facts and Opinions	
I can reflect on my day and week and check my ASD management	Chapters 2 and 3, Reflection	
I know what a healthy lifestyle is for me and practise it	Chapter 5, Healthy Lifestyle	
I can manage situations when they change without having a meltdown or shutdown	Chapter 4, Triggers Solutions Change Triggers Chapter 6, Dealing with Change	
I know about sexual relationships and what makes them safe	Chapter 5, Staying Safe Chapter 6, Friendships	
I know how to choose positive role models and friends and avoid negative relationships	Chapter 6 Friendships	

Skill/Behaviour	Resource /page	Completed date
I have a calm coaching inner voice that encourages me to do great things and helps me deal with challenging situations positively	Chapter 6 Inner Voice Positivity Comfort Zones	
I know my Sensory vulnerabilities and triggers and manage them successfully	Chapter 4 Sensory Triggers & Solutions	
I know what makes me happy and practise these in my daily plan	Chapter 5 Chapter 6 Know myself	
I can conduct a two way conversation by choosing appropriate subjects, asking questions, sharing information and listening and responding	Chapter 6, Rapport, Social Skills	
I can wait my turn and manage my frustrations positively.	Chapter 6, Social Skills, Turn Taking Inner Voice State Management Positivity	
I know when it's good to share and when it's not expected and can assertively share if I choose.	Chapter 6, Social Skills, Sharing, Inner Voice, Assertiveness	

Skill/Behaviour	Resource /page	Completed date
Insert your own behaviours here and below:		

Skill/Behaviour	Resource /page	Completed date

Chapter 7

Summary

This book aims to provide information and tools for Auties who have the ability to understand the concepts and practices listed. The tools can be used over and over again throughout your Autie's lifetime. When your Autie was diagnosed (identified) you may have searched for support and interventions to help and found lots of suggestions and resources, in-fact, too many. This book has been designed so that you can pace your Autie's development whilst prioritising what is important first and leaving the rest until later. The journey may take several years and then continue to need topping up or reminding over the years.

I hope you find these tools and techniques as useful and life changing as I have. I wish you well for your journey in reaching your potential through "downloading grey thinking".

For more information about me and what I do please visit:

www.deemcalinden.weebly.com

Dee McAlinden
Teacher, Tutor, Trainer, Coach, Writer, Public Speaker

Appendices:

Circle of Friends Activity - permission given by the council to use in this book.

LEICESTERSHIRE AUTISM OUTREACH SERVICE

(A Social Skills Programme for Students with Asperger Syndrome in Mainstream Secondary Schools)

Autism Outreach Service Specialist Teaching Services Room 600, Rutland Building County Hall Glenfield Leicestershire LE3 8RA

Service Manager: George Thomas Telephone: 0116 305 9400 e-mail: sts@leics.gov.uk

Guidelines for setting up a Friendship Programme

The Friendship Programme is aimed at students with AS within mainstream secondary placements. Ideally the students should be Year 8 or above, but Year 7 students could take part in the Summer Term. Some of the issues discussed in the programme require a level of maturity that might not be seen in younger students. It is important that the group feel comfortable with each other so it is useful to select students from one tutor group who are familiar with each other.

Group Dynamics: Maximum of six students (even number preferable) – cohort made up of ASD students (maximum of two), other students with social and communication needs; and at least one positive role model who is able to contribute to discussions and behave in an appropriate and mature way during the sessions.

The school will need to send a letter out to the parents of selected students which outlines the intentions of the programme and seeks their permission for the inclusion of their child. An example of this is enclosed.

A space will need to be identified, which is big enough to allow the students to move around freely, isn't overly cluttered with furniture, but has access to chairs, table space and a flip chart, if possible. This space will need to be available each week. This is essential, to allow the programme to run with consistency.

The Friendship Programme is a ten week course that requires an hour for each session. It will be important to identify a slot on the timetable that will allow for the students to be released from an activity e.g. PHSE, PE for the duration of the programme.

The person running the group will require the support of one member of staff, whose role will be to manage students' behaviour, assist with discussions, take part in role-play, and support the students in their activities. This person would need to have a sound understanding of ASD, know the focus student/s well; and feel confident and able to take an active role in the programme.

FRIENDSHIP PROGRAMME

Session One

Introduction:

Adult introduces themselves and the concept of the stress line – lay the rope out on the floor with the flashcards of 'stressed' and 'calm' at either end. Stand at a specific point on the rope to symbolise how you are feeling, and encourage the students to do the same. Adult introduces the programme – The focus is on how we get on with others – ways to make and keep friends, how we sort out problems with friends when they happen

Practicalities of the group – when, where, how many weeks, outline of sessions The sorts of things the group will be doing – games, talking, listening, role-play, relaxation.

Introduce Star Chart System

Explain the star chart system – each person makes a secret vote for the person in the group whom they feel showed the qualities of a good friend, during that friendship session. The person with most votes receives a friendship star, and the person with the most stars at the end of the ten week programme receives a special prize. (Schools could look at how they could support this – perhaps a £5 gift voucher from WH Smith?)

Warm Up Game (see list) – Balloon Game

Chat Time:

Ground rules – Discuss general school rules – who makes them, why we have them etc. Group to devise a list of four/five rules which they all agree to follow each week. Use bank of suggestions to help them to think of their own choices of rules (flashcards – ideas for rules). Display the rules visually on the wall each week. Encourage the group to think about an agreed consequence for breaking the rules. Advise the group that you will make the decisions about behaviour management e.g. when someone needs to take time-out. Advise the group that, if at any time someone feels uncomfortable with a discussion or activity, they may choose to sit and watch.

Activity:

Ice Breakers – Group awareness – standing in order of a) height, b) birthdays, c) initial letter of names, door numbers, the time they got up that morning etc. (Explain the parallel with games – some involve looking, others good listening, sharing information, asking questions etc.) Mime – sharing information about self with the group e.g. favourite activity, favourite food.

Chat time: (carry this over to Week 2 if short of time)

Brainstorm the qualities of a good friend – display on flipchart each week. For example: Kind   Caring Trustworthy Good at sharing Good listener Understand your thoughts and feelings.

Reflection Time:

Ask the group to turn their chairs to face out of the circle. Turn the relaxation music on and encourage the students to think about today's session. Ask them to reflect on who they felt showed the qualities of a good friend, in this session, and how they did that.

Treats or Sweets

Session Two (Ensure the rules, consequences and qualities of a good friend are displayed on the wall)

Warm Up Game – Name 6

Chat Time:

Go over the rules, consequences and qualities of a good friend. Remind students of the voting system.

Identify what makes friendships fun: Shared interests Shared enjoyment of activities Similar sense of humour Feel good about self in friend's company - relaxed, confident, secure Time to talk with someone who thinks about the world in a similar way to you

Brainstorm the positive comments you can make to a friend when playing a game (flashcards – comments and their meanings): For example:

'This is great fun!'   (Showing enthusiasm) 'I'm really enjoying this'   (Sharing positive feelings) 'Come on, Tim - you can do it!'   (Encouraging others) 'Well done, Ann - you did really well!' (Celebrating another's success)

'I didn't do very well - never mind - it's only a game' (Not getting stressed) 'Don't worry Matt - you tried your best' (Boosting someone who hasn't done well) 'It's good to see John and Dan's team winning'   (Allowing others to succeed) 'Do you want to go first or second?'   (Being a good team player)

Ask the group to pair comments with their meanings.

Activity:

Fan the Kipper

Step One: Pair up - one of each partnership to stand at opposite ends of the room from each other. Kipper to be fanned by one partner, across the room to the other partner. This partner then takes over and fans the kipper back to the start. This part of the activity is a competition - to see which partnership wins the race.

Step Two: As a whole group - split the group so that half the students are at one end of the room and half at the other. Kipper to be fanned by player 1 across the room to player 2 who fans it back to player 3 etc. The group have a time limit to see how quickly they can complete the task as a team - this time limit will depend on group size. The group could complete the task again to see if they can beat their previous time.

An alternative to Fan the Kipper could be a Domino race - setting up the dominoes across the room so that when the first one is knocked over, the whole line falls down. Again this could be done in pairs as a race, and then as a whole group against the clock.

As the game is played, encourage the students to make positive comments about their partner/rest of group's contributions to the game and about how they themselves are feeling.

Reflection Time:

Ask the group to turn their chairs to face out of the circle. Turn the relaxation music on and encourage the students to think about today's session. Ask them to reflect on who they felt showed the qualities of a good friend, in this session, and how they did that.

Star Chart

Treats or Sweets

Session Three (Ensure the rules, consequences and qualities of a good friend are displayed on the wall)

Warm Up Game – Fruit Salad

Chat Time:

Discussion on Circles of Friendship and the idea that friendships are flexible:

Use own photos to introduce family and flexibility of friendships.

1) Circles of Friendship (adult to use own friendship circles to demonstrate):

On a flipchart draw three/four concentric circles – two charts which reflect your own circles of friendship – at the age of the students and now. Brainstorm the qualities of friends - the things they do, their personal characteristics. Place own friends on the chart according to the level of intensity of the friendship i.e. close friends near the middle, casual acquaintances further out. Explain the idea that friendship is quite a stretchy term - includes those people we are very close to, and those we would consider to be acquaintances. Stress that all are forms of friendship. Brainstorm the students' ideas of who would be a close friend and who would be a casual acquaintance.

2) Flexibility of Friendships:

Emphasise that all forms of friendship are equally valid and important to us. Also reassure that some of us may be quite happy just to have the sort of relationships characteristic of the outer circle. Discuss the idea of friendships changing - some develop and some fade. Use own friendship circles to demonstrate this idea of flexibility (e.g. losing friends after leave school, developing new friends in the workplace). Encourage students to share how they feel when they lose friends or feel unable to make friends - lonely, sad, cross. Again, use own experiences to show the students how these feelings are experienced by everyone at some point in their life as friendships change.

Group draw their own circles of friendship and share with each other.

Activity:

Chair Game: 1) Paired task – each pairing, using two chairs, are to get from one side of the room to the other without touching the floor. Adult to supervise but not offer solutions. Adult can call 'freeze' at any time to ask students how they are feeling (frustrated, confident etc.).

2) Whole group task – the whole group are to get from one side of the room to the other using chairs (one less than the group size), without touching the floor. As before, the adult will call 'freeze' to discuss feelings, the ideas of compromise and negotiation; and teamwork.

This activity does raise the issue of Health and Safety. If it is not appropriate to use chairs, please substitute with sheets of newspaper.

Reflection Time:

Ask the group to turn their chairs to face out of the circle. Turn the relaxation music on and encourage the students to think about today's session. Ask them to reflect on who they felt showed the qualities of a good friend, in this session, and how they did that.

Star Chart

Treats or Sweets

Session Four (Ensure the rules, consequences and qualities of a good friend are displayed on the wall)

Warm Up Game – Stick Game

Chat Time: Discuss the idea of feeling rejected by a friend. When can these situations arise e.g. playground, dining hall, PE? Identify the feelings associated with this - angry thoughts, feelings of loss, stress, and upset. Stress especially the temptation to punish/take it out on your friend or others. Brainstorm the reasons why you might feel rejected by someone, although that person may still be a friend. Look at self-talk statements which could help to repair the negative feelings (flashcards – self-talk statements to cope with feeling rejected) e.g.

They didn't realise how much you wanted to play. They needed a bit of a change. They have several friends and it's OK for them to play with others. They had other stuff on their mind. They weren't in the mood I arrived late in the dining hall so there was no room left at the table.

Use role-play to rehearse situations and responses to feeling rejected.

Activity:

What's in the Bag? Each student in turn puts their hand in the bag and 1) describes what they feel, 2) describes what they see and 3) describes its function. Others to guess. At the end, make reference to friendships and how it is important to know more about a friend than just what they look like.

Reflection Time:

Ask the group to turn their chairs to face out of the circle. Turn the relaxation music on and encourage the students to think about today's session. Ask them to reflect on who they felt showed the qualities of a good friend, in this session, and how they did that.

Star Chart

Treats or Sweets

Session Five (Ensure the rules, consequences and qualities of a good friend are displayed on the wall)

Warm Up Game – Lid Game

Chat Time:

Encourage students to identify situations where they have either: a) put themselves down when they've made a mistake, or b) talked themselves into a rage because others have been teasing. Identify the negative thoughts that we have in situations like these and how they have a significant role in making matters worse. Discuss the idea of self-talk – positive statements (flashcards – positive statements to boost self-esteem) that we can say to ourselves which will boost our self-esteem and reinforce self-control e.g.

It doesn't matter if I make a mistake – this is new. When I learn something new it's OK to make mistakes. Everybody makes mistakes sometimes. I'm not going to let him get to me. I can handle this. I'm not giving YOU the pleasure of making ME lose my temper.

Discuss calming down techniques – what do you do?

Activity:

Divide the group in half and ask pairings to sit opposite their partner (3 facing 3). Put a picture up on the wall behind one group of three, who have a blank piece of paper and a pencil. The other partner's role is to describe the picture, which they are facing, to their partner, who cannot see it but will attempt to draw it. This partner is not allowed to name any objects from picture, but to use good describing words and directions to ensure picture drawn reflects picture displayed on the wall.

Reflection Time:

Ask the group to turn their chairs to face out of the circle. Turn the relaxation music on and encourage the students to think about today's session. Ask them to reflect on who they felt showed the qualities of a good friend, in this session, and how they did that.

Star Chart

Treats or Sweets

Session Six (Ensure the rules, consequences and qualities of a good friend are displayed on the wall)

Warm Up Game – Change It

Chat Time:

Introduce the idea of conflict – ask the students to share their ideas and opinions of what this is. Introduce the idea of conflict within a friendship – encourage students to think of situations which may damage a friendship. Discuss 'explosion' point – use of stress rope to encourage students to talk about either how they feel right then or what would put them at the stressed/calm ends of the rope. Briefly mention the concept of finding a middle way or a resolution that: a) defuses b) avoids escalation c) causes least damage to the friendship. Role play or use video footage to look at different scenarios involving conflict. Look at different ways of resolving these situations (flashcards – resolution of conflict) e.g.

Walk away, hit out force him to play your way, threaten never to play with him again or not to be his friend, put your hand over your ears, try to compromise – so long your way, so long my way – a 'middle ground'. Suggest an alternative that might be OK for both of you. Try out his way and re-assure yourself. Use a script e.g. 'It's not worth falling out over this'.

Discuss the pros and cons of the above list and identify the most appropriate to use.

Activity:

Construction Task – to encourage co-operation (working together towards a shared goal).

Equipment – large box of Lego or any other construction toys

Task – Players have to work together to build a construction, but one which develops as they go along, rather than setting out with a specific end in mind. Each participant has to make a link between what he does on his turn and what the person before him did

e.g. I used the same shape/colour block, I used the same size, I put it next to yours, and I kept building in the same direction.

Encourage others to acknowledge the contribution and the way it has added to the construction e.g. it's made it bigger, it's made it stronger, it's made it taller, and it looks more interesting.

Alternative activity – drawing a picture as a group. The group share a packet of pens and one large piece of paper. Using the same concepts as for the construction task they need to produce one picture.

Reflection Time:

Ask the group to turn their chairs to face out of the circle. Turn the relaxation music on and encourage the students to think about today's session. Ask them to reflect on who they felt showed the qualities of a good friend, in this session, and how they did that.

Star Chart

Treats or Sweets

Session Seven (Ensure the rules, consequences and qualities of a good friend are displayed on the wall)

Warm Up Game – Chinese Whispers

Chat Time:

Look at the concepts of compromise and negotiation – use the dictionary to define. Use the 'donkey' picture to help to explain compromise. Review the idea of compromise and negotiation from the last session. - Explain how these skills help to maintain a friendship during times of possible conflict. - Discuss possible situations where compromise and negotiation would be necessary.

Learning how to lose gracefully: - Discuss what it means to be a sore loser (someone who always has to win to feel good). Explain that having friends means learning how to lose without ruining the enjoyment of a game for your partners.

Activity:

Use any simple game that has winners and losers and can be conducted rapidly e.g. Snap, musical chairs.

1) The first time the game is played, the object is to purposely try to lose. Tell the students that you want to see how fast they can lose without cheating. The idea is for them to feel relaxed about losing. Freeze the game at any time to discuss how the students feel about losing. Encourage them to make positive comments to each other

about their participation. Discuss whether it really matters that they have lost.

2) The second time the game is played, the object is to win. Tell the students that they are now to play the game properly, trying to win. Freeze the game at any time to discuss how the students feel about winning. How does the winner appear to others?

Reflection Time:

Ask the group to turn their chairs to face out of the circle. Turn the relaxation music on and encourage the students to think about today's session. Ask them to reflect on who they felt showed the qualities of a good friend, in this session, and how they did that.

Star Chart

Treats or Sweets

Session Eight (Ensure the rules, consequences and qualities of a good friend are displayed on the wall)

Warm Up Game – Electric Chair Game

Chat Time:

Discuss 'teasing' and what the students' understanding of this is. Encourage students to share their experiences. Brainstorm different scenarios and identify which would be (flashcards – different levels of teasing):

Gentle teasing (from a friend/relative who is just joking with you) Cruel teasing (from someone who is deliberately trying to hurt/anger you) Dangerous teasing (from someone who is trying to wind you up so that the situation will become aggressive and someone may get hurt/in trouble).

Use role-play to rehearse different kinds of teasing.

Discuss things others might do which would upset us: - Making us feel stupid - making us feel that everyone is looking or laughing at us - making us feel that the Mickey has been taken out of something or someone that is important to us.

Discuss why reacting can often make matters worse, even if we are in the right. Look at what is involved in ignoring/not reacting to teasing. Practise the appropriate facial expression and posture which would reflect the thoughts 'this really isn't very interesting' or 'I can hardly be bothered'. Rehearse the self-talk script - 'I'm not rising to the bait' (or something similar). Think of ways of putting the other person down (in your head).

Explore the idea of going too far - how you have to monitor a friend's reaction to check that they really do find the gentle teasing funny. Discuss how too much of a good thing can cause a friend to feel irritated/upset by you.

Activity:

Play a selection of silly games e.g. twister, electric chair game, stuck in the mud etc. to rehearse the idea of having fun with your friends without going too far.

Reflection Time:

Ask the group to turn their chairs to face out of the circle. Turn the relaxation music on and encourage the students to think about today's session. Ask them to reflect on who they felt showed the qualities of a good friend, in this session, and how they did that.

Star Chart

Treats or Sweets

Session Nine (Ensure the rules, consequences and qualities of a good friend are displayed on the wall).

Warm Up Game – Pass the Koosh, Balloon Game, Students' own request

Chat Time:

Staying Connected Brainstorm the ways we stay connected to others. Discuss the importance of staying connected with our friends – keeping in touch, holding connected conversations, sharing things in common etc.

Cartoon Strips: Use cards to arrange pairings, to avoid focus student from being left out. In pairs, complete the four square cartoon strip staying connected with the picture in box 1. As a pair, discuss the topic of box 1, make decisions about who draws, what to draw, topic for boxes two to four, speech bubbles etc. Present to the group and discuss.

Activity:

Paired task – Blindfold rope shapes

Equipment – one long piece of rope and one scarf (per pair). Task – one student in each pair wears a blindfold. The other student verbally directs them in creating different shapes with the rope on the floor e.g. circle, square, triangle, star etc. The students will swap over half way through so that both have experienced the difficulties of a) not being able to see, and b) modifying their language effectively. Aim – the student giving the instructions will modify their use of language to ensure that they give clear, explicit instructions to their blindfolded partner. This will reduce feelings of frustration during the activity. The 'seeing' partner may need some support in order to think about ways of conveying what they mean to their partner.

Ask students to describe the skills involved in the game.

Reflection Time:

Ask the group to turn their chairs to face out of the circle. Turn the relaxation music on and encourage the students to think about today's session. Ask them to reflect on who they felt showed the qualities of a good friend, in this session, and how they did that.

Star Chart

Treats or Sweets

Session Ten (Ensure the rules, consequences and qualities of a good friend are displayed on the wall)

Warm Up Game – Who's In the Bag?

Chat Time:

1) Review the Friendship Programme - encourage the students to think about the skills they have practised and to identify one thing they have learned which they feel they could take away and use in everyday situations. 2) Questionnaire for students and staff to complete – feedback for AOT.

Activity:

Coming up with new ideas together

To rehearse a variety of skills learned throughout the programme - taking turns, sharing, finding a middle ground, negotiating, valuing the contributions of your partner, being a friend.

- two piles of cards with animal pictures. - Students work in pairs (use cards to organise). Each pairing chooses a card from each pile. The pairing has to combine the two animals into a new, imaginary animal and decide on: its name, where it lives, what it will look like (blend of the two sets of features), what it eats, what it does all day, what it is scared of, what skills it has etc.

- Each pairing then shares their new creation with the rest of the group.

Reflection Time:

Ask the group to turn their chairs to face out of the circle. Turn the relaxation music on and encourage the students to think about today's session. Ask them to reflect on who they felt showed the qualities of a good friend, in this session, and how they did that.

Friendship Star Award Certificates

Friendship Star

Student Good Friend

Tick the box of the person you think has shown the qualities of a good friend this week.

You cannot vote for yourself!

Friendship Star

Student Good Friend

Tick the box of the person you think has shown the qualities of a good friend this week.

You cannot vote for yourself!

Friendship Star

Proforma – Letter to Parents (on school's letter head)

Dear -----------------

Philip Whitaker (Senior Educational Psychologist) and staff from the Specialist Teaching Service have developed a social communication programme that identifies and addresses key areas of difficulty in relation to building and maintaining friendships. They have felt that this work is particularly important in the secondary school environment where students can feel increasingly socially isolated from their peers. The Friendship Programme also helps students to feel more confident in their own ability and encourages the development of a positive self-esteem.

The Friendship Programme has been running in a number of secondary schools throughout Leicestershire since 2004, with great success. We should like to run the programme here at -------------------- and are requesting your permission for ------------------------- to take part in the group *(as a positive role model for some less able students)*. It will run for a course of ten weeks, starting on -------------- . The students will be released from their ------------- lesson each -------------- (day/time) to attend the group.

Should you have any queries or concerns about this programme please do not hesitate to contact ------------ at ---------------- School. Thank you for your support.

Kindest Regards

SENCo/teacher School

*delete as appropriate

Resources List

Every week:

Flipchart (at least A3 size) Blu Tac Marker pens Koosh ball or other object to use as focus for listening and turn-taking CD player Relaxation CD Length of rope (stress rope) Flashcards – stressed and calm Star chart Voting sheets Sticky stars Box of sweets

Week One: Flashcards – ideas for rules

Week Two: Flipchart – friendship group rules, consequences, and qualities of a good friend Flashcards – positive comments to make to a friend during a game. Flashcards – the meaning behind the positive comments. Kippers – made from aluminium foil. Fans e.g. newspaper/books

Week Three: Flipchart – friendship group rules, consequences, and qualities of a good friend your own circles of friendship charts and photos

Week Four: Flipchart – friendship group rules, consequences, and qualities of a good friend Flashcards – self-talk statements to cope with feeling rejected. two bags, with a selection of everyday objects e.g. light bulb, mobile phone, pastry brush, battery, hoover attachment, CD etc. Lined paper and pens for the students.

Week Five: Flipchart – friendship group rules, consequences, and qualities of a good friend Flashcards – positive statements to boost self-esteem. A4 blank paper and pencils two pictures for activity

Week Six:

Flipchart – friendship group rules, consequences, and qualities of a good friend Flashcards – resolution of conflict Construction toy e.g. Lego or Piece of flipchart and coloured pens

Week Seven: Flipchart – friendship group rules, consequences, and qualities of a good friend Game to experience losing. Donkey picture Dictionary

Week Eight: Flipchart – friendship group rules, consequences, and qualities of a good friend Flashcards – different levels of teasing

Week Nine: Flipchart – friendship group rules, consequences, and qualities of a good friend Cartoon strips – four boxes, first one with scenario drawn e.g. making a mistake, being rejected, conflict etc. Pens and pencil three blindfolds three lengths of rope

Week Ten: Flipchart – friendship group rules, consequences, and qualities of a good friend Pictures of animals A4 blank paper Pens Questionnaires – for students and staff Certificates Special prize for friendship star winner

Ideas for Warm-Up Games

Stick Game Choose the stick or scarf, or both, and use actions to turn them into something else e.g. making the stick a toothbrush. (Encourages imagination, turn-taking, shared focus).

Fruit Salad Sit in circle with one chair short in circle – that person stands in the middle. Each person is given a fruit name (use three different fruits) and when the person in the middle calls your fruit; everyone who is the same fruit must swap seats. The person in the middle must try to gain a seat, and the person who is without a seat stands in the middle for the next turn. If 'fruit salad' is called, everyone must swap seats. (Encourages focus, spatial awareness, good listening).

Balloon Game Hit balloon around the circle to introduce self to the group. Extend to swap seats by calling out another person's name when you hit the balloon. (Helps to establish names in a fun way and encourages awareness of others, good looking, and memory for names).

Pass Game Pass a bean bag or Koosh ball around the circle to share information e.g. likes and dislikes. (Encourages shared focus, sharing of information, turn-taking).

Chinese Whispers Pass a whispered message around the circle and see whether it remains accurate by the time it returns to the first person. (Encourages good listening and tolerance of close proximity).

Who's in the Bag? Split the group in to two teams – take turns to pick a card from the bag and describe the person named on the card to their team, without naming them. See how many they can do in one minute. After everyone has had a turn, the team with the most cards wins. (Encourages the use of good descriptive language, performance skills, focus of attention,

Name 6 Sit in circle with one person sitting in the middle. In the time it takes to pass a koosh ball around the circle, the person in the middle tries to name six agreed objects e.g. six animals, six countries beginning with 'a'. Swap around. (Encourages turn-taking, awareness of others, knowledge of the world, focus and speed).

Lid Game An individual is presented with a number of bottles and jars and a pile of lids. In one minute they must try to put as many lids as possible on the correct bottle/jar. (Encourages fine motor skills, and gives the experience of losing).

Change It One person leaves the room. While they are out of the room one person in the group changes something about their appearance e.g. takes off a sweater, pulls up their sleeves. The person returns and attempts to identify what has changed. The game can be extended by more than one person changing their appearance. (Encourages observational skills and focus of attention).

Electric Chair Game - The group stand in a circle holding hands, around an empty chair. On the word 'go' the group attempt to manoeuvre their peers to touch the chair. Any student who touches the chair must leave the game, until only one person remains. The game can be extended by organising the group to stand in the circle with their backs to the chair. (Gives the experience of 'going too far' and wanting to win, as well as tolerance of close proximity).

Made in the USA
Columbia, SC
20 April 2017